HERNDON DAVIS

HERNDON

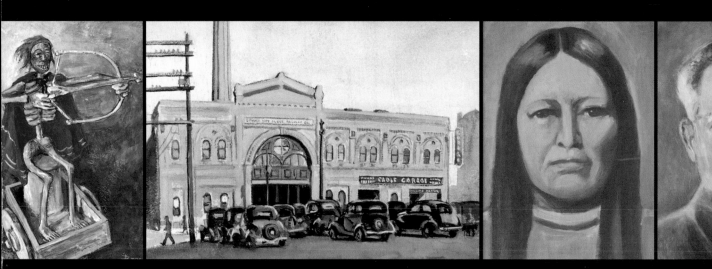

DAVIS

PAINTING COLORADO HISTORY, 1901–1962

CRAIG W. LEAVITT AND THOMAS J. NOEL

UNIVERSITY PRESS OF COLORADO
Boulder

THE CENTER FOR COLORADO AND THE WEST AT AURARIA LIBRARY
DENVER PUBLIC LIBRARY WESTERN HISTORY AND GENEALOGY DEPARTMENT

Published by University Press of Colorado
5589 Arapahoe Avenue, Suite 206C
Boulder, Colorado 80303

 The University Press of Colorado is a proud member of
the Association of American University Presses.

The University Press of Colorado is a cooperative publishing enter-
prise supported, in part, by Adams State University, Colorado State
University, Fort Lewis College, Metropolitan State University of
Denver, Regis University, University of Colorado, University of
Northern Colorado, Utah State University, and Western State Colorado
University.

∞ This paper meets the requirements of the ANSI/NISO Z39.48-1992
(Permanence of Paper).

ISBN: 978-1-60732-419-5 (cloth)
ISBN: 978-1-60732-420-1 (ebook)

Library of Congress Cataloging-in-Publication Data

Leavitt, Craig W., author.
  Herndon Davis : painting Colorado history, 1901–1962 / By Craig W.
Leavitt & Thomas J. Noel.
    pages cm
  Includes bibliographical references.
  ISBN 978-1-60732-419-5 (cloth) — ISBN 978-1-60732-420-1 (ebook)
1. Davis, Herndon, 1901–1962. 2. Artists—United States—Biography.
3. Davis, Herndon, 1901–1962—Themes, motives. 4. Colorado—In
art. I. Noel, Thomas J. (Thomas Jacob), author. II. Title.
  N6537.D3445L43 2015
  759.13—dc23
  [B]
                                    2015014120

Cover and text design by Daniel Pratt

25 24 23 22 21 20 19 18 17 16   10 9 8 7 6 5 4 3 2 1

CREDITS

To all the artists, past, present, and future, who capture and share the beauty of Colorado and the West.

— CL

For my beloved wife and confidante, Vi.

— TN

THE ART OF HERNDON

PEOPLE | 15

PLACES | 177

SANTOS

PLACES

OTHER WORKS

Housed in the Western History and Genealogy Department is one of our most prized treasures, the Herndon Davis collection of paintings and drawings. Anyone dealing with notable characters and locations in Colorado can explore Davis's artwork, which, in some cases, provides the only extant images of certain people and buildings. His many colorful paintings and drawings add impressively to our historic gallery of twentieth-century Colorado as well as to our collection of religious santo images. The Denver Public Library is pleased to be both a collaborator and sponsor on this overdue book on one of our most popular and prolific artists.

Published to coincide with the Denver Public Library's 2016 exhibition—the only civic display of Davis's work to date—and bringing deserved attention to this overlooked figure, *Herndon Davis: Painting Colorado History, 1901–1962* is a significant contribution to Colorado's cultural and visual history.

Circus clowns and elephants and bareback horse riders, glamorous Florodora Girls, horse and dog races, boxers, scenes of the Bowery . . . to my young imagination, the basement walls in the Ritter home were covered and alive with Herndon Davis murals.

Anyone who dreams of creating a book should be sincerely grateful to those who agree to author and sponsor the book. Without their resources, talents, and experience, this book would not be possible. Also, today's digital technologies bring to the book's printed pages a vast collection of images for Herndon Davis's paintings and murals. The Ritter murals are the seed that led to my decision to originate this book. These friends of my parents commissioned Herndon Davis to paint murals of some favorite themes in the basement of their Denver home. When the home was to be razed, I arranged for the murals to be photographed, and a videotape was created. Years later, worrying about the tape in my closet, I mentioned Herndon Davis to Tom Noel and was delighted that he quickly shared my enthusiasm.

So, I first thank Tom "Dr. Colorado" Noel, Denver's beloved historian and author, for sharing my dream for this book about Herndon Davis, a twentieth-century historian with a paint brush. University of Colorado Denver History Fellow and author Craig Leavitt's thorough research and talented writing make this book a delight. Craig and Tom captioned the many images, explaining their significance. Tom Noel and Mary Somerville, co-directors of the Center for Colorado and the West at the Auraria Library, graciously co-sponsored the book. Tom and Craig's research led to the treasure trove of Herndon Davis paintings and drawings in the archives of the Denver Public Library, which generously co-sponsored both the book and a related exhibit at the Central Library. I will always remember the magical morning with Tom and Craig as Jim Kroll showed us DPL's collection of Herndon Davis's beautiful and detailed paintings of now historic characters, places, and other subjects, from saints to dinosaurs. History Colorado also shared its important collection. So, this book fulfills my dream of a comprehensive biography of Herndon Davis and presents a comprehensive collection of his fascinating images.

"Oh yeah, wasn't he that guy who painted *The Face on the Barroom Floor* up in Central City at the Teller House Bar?" Few people realize that Colorado artist Herndon Davis was much more than that. He captured the people and places of the Old West transitioning to modern times. His fascination with the human face is epitomized by that lovely visage on the floor of what is now called the Face Bar. Probably a million people have stared into her big brown eyes.

Herndon painted her in 1936 when the Central City Opera House Association commissioned him to do a series of portraits. The face supposedly belongs to Herndon's wife, Juanita, who looks a little skeptical about being the model. But her visage has become legendary and even launched a popular one-act play, *The Face on the Barroom Floor,* which the Central City Opera House Association first produced in 1978 and occasionally repeats to this day.

Miraculously, the face on the saloon floor survives, although much of Davis's painting is gone. His murals in the Tea Room of the Denver Dry Goods Store are no more, although the building, restored, still stands. Also vanished is A. B. Wade's Keg Bar on 18th Street, where Davis painted faces of prominent Denver folks on the seats so bar flies could sit on their faces. Vanished as well are the murals once in the Hilltop neighborhood basement of the Ritter home that inspired Diane Wunnicke to make this book happen. Diane at least rescued some photos of the Ritter murals included in this book.

Diane conceived of and financed this project. The bulk of the research and writing fell on the strong shoulders of Craig W. Leavitt, a star fellow at the Center for Colorado and the West at the Auraria Library. Operations there are ably led by Dr. Mary M. Somerville, chief librarian and financial wizard.

At History Colorado, photo archivist Melissa Van Otterloo and staff photographer Jay DiLorenzo aided our attempt to locate and procure reproductions of every Herndon Davis work that could be found. Jay provided considerable time, trouble, and expertise to capture the many endangered photos in the basement of the former Denver home of Davis patron Fred Mazzulla. At the Western History and Genealogy Department of the Denver Public Library, a haven for researchers that is also a great center for local art, Manager Jim Kroll spent days digging out Davis's work and guiding us through those well-preserved treasures. DPL's photo librarian Coi Gehrig likewise did heroic work in aiding our search. Hugh Grant at the Kirkland Museum of Fine and Decorative Art, which does a fabulous job of collecting and celebrating Colorado artists, lent a hand. So did Thomas Smith at the Denver Art Museum and Alan Kania, historian of the Denver Press Club.

Who knows how many other walls were or perhaps are still adorned by the work of Colorado's most ubiquitous artist. Fortunately, you can still find his portraits of important founding fathers of Colorado in the Sage Room of the Oxford Hotel at 17th and Wazee Streets. These worthies were salvaged from the Windsor Hotel at 18th and Larimer Streets on the eve of its 1960 demolition.

The Denver Press Club at 1330 Glenarm Place still treasures Davis's work on its basement poker room walls. That large mural depicts the 1940s Press Room of the *Rocky Mountain News*, a place Davis frequented and where he worked. Among the immortals whose heads Davis painted on the outer edges of the mural are longtime favorite *Rocky Mountain News* columnist Lew Casey (editor of the book *Denver Murders*) and *News* photographer Harry Rhoads (the most famous and ribald of the press photographers, whose work is preserved in a biography and in the Western History and Genealogy Department of the Denver Public Library). On that same Denver Press Club mural, look for Gene Fowler, the *Denver Post* reporter who graduated to the big time and national fame in New York City. Among Fowler's many books is one of the liveliest accounts in Denver literature, *Timberline: A Story of Bonfils and Tammen*. More than just a history of the founders of the *Denver Post*, this is a colorful, if not always factual, history of Colorado. It portrays in print the wild, funny, vividly colorful good old days that much of Herndon Davis's work captures. Presumably, the Denver Press Club Davis murals are safe. That fortress claims to be the oldest continuous surviving press club in America and is a designated Denver landmark. And its inner sanctum's most treasured relic is the Herndon Davis mural.

In numerous projects, Davis gave faces to famous western characters, creating alternative images to the scant black-and-white photos extant for many important characters and structures. Davis often revived faces and places in full color, basing his portrait on the black-and-white photos available or on the person or place if he knew them. His memorable watercolors of Denver's fading Tabor Grand Opera House and the former Mattie Silks bordello, for instance, captured their sad decline. With unflinching realism, Davis includes the automobiles, the clothing, the background pedestrians and signage that make his cityscapes unforgettable, colorful period pieces.

In at least one case, Davis gave a face to a theretofore faceless hero. John H. Gregory, a key figure in the 1859 Colorado gold rush who discovered the first mother lode. An experienced gold miner from Georgia, Gregory knew the placer gold everyone else was fishing for in rivers and creeks had come from underground veins upstream. On May 6, 1859, he opened the Gregory lode along what is now Gregory Gulch, which flows between what quickly became Central City and Black Hawk. After making that discovery, which saved a sputtering gold rush, Gregory mysteriously disappeared. Not even an image could be found until Davis, using historical written descriptions, produced a portrait of a shaggy miner with a beard thick enough to hide mice.

As this book's superb biography of Davis by Craig W. Leavitt reveals, he was far more than the tipsy artist who painted *The Face on the Barroom Floor*. Somehow, Davis has never attracted artistic scrutiny or been the subject of any biography longer than a newspaper article. Yet he captured better than any other artist the many faces and places most notable in Colorado history. Art historians may dismiss his work, but anyone interested in Colorado history should rejoice in this gifted artist who resurrected so much of our past with his pencils, brushes, and pen and ink.

HERNDON DAVIS

Herndon Richard Davis was born on October 27, 1901, in Wynnewood, Oklahoma. A child of the transitional West, his long artistic career reflected both the romanticized West of the popular imagination and the real-life struggles of a region adapting to the rapid economic changes of the first half of the twentieth century. Davis was more than a "Western" artist. Before he settled into his role as unofficial "painter laureate" of the West, as famed military illustrator Ernie Pyle called him, Davis had already won the praise of generals, governors, and presidents for his uncannily accurate and sensitive portraits.[1] While still in his twenties, he had portrayed kings, movie stars, and legendary sports champions for millions of newspaper readers in America's biggest media markets. His work earned the validation of critics and academics; it hung in prestigious Manhattan galleries.

Davis grew up in Oklahoma and could boast that his grandfather was first cousin to Confederate president Jefferson Davis. His parents, far from successful ranchers and farmers, moved the family thirteen times in as many years. Young Herndon began sketching as a toddler. In later life he claimed he "could plow a pretty good furrow," but he admitted to hating milking cows.[2] The farming life was not for him.

Art seems to have always been a part of Davis's family life. Correspondence to and from both his mother and his wife was heavily illustrated with whimsical cartoons and sketches, mostly of animals. The earliest document of Davis's life found in his papers at the Denver Public Library Western History and Genealogy Department archive is a homemade Valentine's Day card to his mother, dated February 14, 1909, from her seven-year-old son. The paper valentine is adorned with a drawing of a lady in a blue coat, her face covered by a pink hood. Art was not just a vocation or a career for Herndon. It became part of the fabric and currency of his everyday life.

Surviving early works by Davis show the development of his artistic gift. A charcoal self-portrait done when Davis was twelve years old, in 1914, reveals his sensitivity to human personalities, including his own. A reporter profiling Davis as a mature artist later wrote: "When he cartoons himself, Herndon is merciless. He exaggerates his strong nose into an aggressive hook; the character lines which accent his cheeks and underscore his fine eyes become the lines of a rather solemn buffoon under his own brutal pencil . . . [His] generosity and kindly attitude are extended to all but himself."[3] But in the childhood self-portrait, the young artist granted himself the dignity his portraits would give to many others in the coming years. The picture reveals an earnest, intelligent soul with thoughtful, clear eyes that seemed already to see deeply into the world around them.

After leaving his parents' farm at age fourteen, Davis headed to Kansas City, Missouri, where he shined shoes to earn money for his first art lessons. His first art-related jobs were in Chicago, where he served as an engraver's apprentice and worked as a commercial artist for Armour and Company, the giant meat-packing firm. In 1918 he harvested fields to fund a short stint at William Jewell College in Liberty, Kansas. Davis first visited

Denver in 1920 as a US Army private, with troops stationed in the Mile High City to keep the peace during the Denver Tramway Company streetcar workers' strike. The army recognized Davis's artistic talent and fostered it, employing him in Washington, DC, as a drafter of secret military maps of Japan and China. He studied at the War College and the Corcoran School of Fine Art, and briefly, in 1925, he did a stint at Yale, which he was unable to continue because of a lack of funds. Around this time, Davis's great facility for capturing character in the human face became evident in his work. His friendly and outgoing nature helped bring portrait commissions from the high-ranking military officers who were also his drinking buddies. Rear Admiral Franklin J. Drake, a descendent of famed English seaman Sir Francis Drake, was so taken by the young artist from Oklahoma who did his portrait that he willed Davis all his dress uniforms.[4]

By the late 1920s Davis was living in New York City's Greenwich Village, where he took classes at the Art Students League and the National Academy Museum, earning his school fees by drawing pastels of burlesque queens. Davis was also a prolific commercial illustrator during his New York years. His drawings appeared in the *New York Herald-Tribune*, the *Washington Times-Herald,* and the *Washington Daily News* (where he worked with the famous army illustrator Ernie Pyle), as well as *Forum* and *McClure's* magazines. In 1929 he met Edna Juanita Cotter, another Greenwich Village artist who lived in the same apartment building as Davis. "Nita" was a British subject from Jamaica and eleven years his senior. Like him an artist, she specialized in hand-painted Christmas cards. Soon, they married.

Davis made a powerful reputation for himself on the East Coast. His work in the army opened many doors and put Davis in the presence of some of the great figures of twentieth-century American history. He portrayed famous people living and dead and evoked grateful and enthusiastic responses from his subjects and patrons. General Douglas MacArthur and New York governor Franklin D. Roosevelt personally acknowledged Davis's portraits of themselves with thank you notes. During this period, Davis also received congratulatory letters from the National Geographic Society, the American Museum of Natural History, and numerous highly placed military and political figures.

A letter dated July 26, 1926, from Mrs. Florence Jackson Stoddard, founder of the International Association of Art and Letters in Washington, DC, praised Davis for his rendering of her famous forebear. "I can tell you only lamely that the pleasure you have given me in presenting to me your wonderful pen-painting of my great kinsman, Andrew Jackson, the seventh president of this our native land, is really quite inexpressible," wrote Mrs. Stoddard. "This picture is to go to you or your heirs when I shall have departed to that place where, perhaps, I may see face to face the hero whose features you here have limned."[5] Whether Stoddard's pledge to have the work returned after her death was ever fulfilled is unknown.

The front page of the *New York Evening Post* reported on December 8, 1926, that "Corporal Herndon R. Davis, stationed at Fort Jay, Governors Island, has done pen and ink drawing of sufficient merit to win him a 'show' in an uptown gallery."[6] The show at the Knoedler Gallery in Manhattan included Davis's rendering of General Charles P. Summerall, who had led US forces on the front lines during World War I and served as army chief of staff from 1926 to 1930. The article featured a photograph of the rumpled artist himself rather than one of his works. The *Post* story was syndicated nationwide, putting Davis's face on the covers of the *Boston Traveler* (December 9), the *New York Times* (December 16), and the *Los Angeles Illustrated Daily News* (December 31).

Military work continued to garner acclaim for Davis. The *St. Louis Globe Democrat* editorial page on August 16, 1927, praised a traveling exhibition of "almost 100 posters and photographs describing educational work, travel and sports of the army." According to the *Globe Democrat*, "One of the notable original sketches is one of Charles Lindbergh, a pen and ink drawing made by Herndon R. Davis, United States Army, which has been reproduced in a poster and distributed from one end of the country to another."[7]

Adjutant General I. J. Phillipson wrote on May 21, 1927, of Davis's "splendid pen portrait of President Coolidge," adding "if the opportunity presents itself, the General will present the picture to the President."[8] Major General J. H. McRae wrote to the artist on November 29, 1927, thanking him for the "excellent work you are doing for the Recruiting Publicity Bureau. I also want to thank you for the splendid portrait which you recently made and presented to me . . . as good [as] or perhaps better than any photograph taken of me in recent years."[9] Davis contributed a number of military portraits, including that of Lindbergh, to the premier issue of *Our Army* magazine in 1928. A letter dated October 29, 1928, from Lieutenant Colonel G. V. Heidt of the War Department's Recruiting Publicity Bureau praised the "splendid" drawing of Lindbergh by "Sergeant Davis"—who had evidently been promoted for his excellent work since appearing in newspapers nationwide as Corporal Davis in 1926.[10]

It must be a testament to Herndon's attachment to Denver and Colorado that he continued to gravitate to the Centennial State despite opportunities elsewhere. He earned his bona fides as a westerner when he participated as a staff artist in a 1933 expedition to explore Yampa Canyon in northwest Colorado. Davis's expedition art appeared two years later in a feature for the *Washington Post* entitled "Yampa Canyon, America's Last Bit of Wild West." Described as "one of the most important members of the expedition," Davis drew "cowboy portraits" and made a visual record of the remote and exotic western landscapes he and his companions encountered.[11] When a rattlesnake menaced the group, "Davis killed it with a well-aimed shot from his revolver," like a seasoned western pioneer.[12] In addition to Davis's six-shooter heroics, the trip yielded an impressionistic watercolor work called *Junction Yampa and Hell's Canyon*, which is now part of the Denver Public Library's cache of Davis originals.

A *Washington Post* article spotlighting staff artist Herndon Davis, published November 16, 1934, gives fascinating insight into the artist's technique as well as the high regard for Davis at the peak of his East Coast career:

The unique style used by Herndon Davis in the pen portraits which appear in the Washington Post has inspired Prof. Sydney W. Little, of the Department of Architecture at Clemson College, South Carolina, to ask for a collection of originals to be loaned as an exhibit for art students in the college to study. While Mr. Davis does wash or brush drawings which are widely known for their excellence, his pen portraits have brought him still greater renown, because it is a style which he himself developed. You will find one of these portraits any Sunday on the drama page. Take a close look at one of them, and you will be interested in the unusual style in which they are executed, each formed of cross strokes of the pen, larger and smaller, lighter and darker, to achieve the effect desired.

Mr. Davis is nationally recognized for his work. One art critic has said that he is the only man who paints true portraits with his pen. Another stated that there are only four outstanding and original pen techniques in the country, developed by these four artists; Walter Teague, Rockwell Kent, Franklin Booth, and Herndon Davis.

In the rush of getting out a newspaper, Mr. Davis has developed remarkable speed in doing his pen portraits. However, when he sits down to do one that is so perfect as to suit him in every detail, it takes a full week. Once, Mr. Davis says, curiosity impelled him to start counting the number of cross strokes he makes in one portrait, but his patience was not sufficient and he gave up. It's work enough to do them, he says, without counting them besides.[13]

It is unclear how or why Davis stopped drawing for the *Washington Post* and other eastern periodicals. He may have been a victim of Depression-era belt-tightening. Or he may simply have wanted to renew his roots in the West. According to the chronology he supplied to the *Denver Post* in a 1954 interview, Davis and his wife, Nita, came to visit his mother in Denver in 1936. "That is a polite way of saying that an unemployed newspaper artist from Washington D.C. came home to eat," he told the *Post* with characteristic self-effacing humor.[14] Whatever the reason for his return to the West, it led to the creation of his most famous and distinctive work, *The Face on the Barroom Floor*, at the Teller House Bar in Central City.

As Davis himself told it:

The Central City Opera House Association hired me to do a series of paintings and sketches of the famous mountain town, which they were then rejuvenating as an opera center and tourist attraction.

I stayed at the Teller House while working up there, and the whim struck me to paint a face on the floor of the old Teller House barroom. In its mining boom heyday it was just such a floor as the ragged artist used in H. Antoine d'Arcy's famous old poem.

But the hotel manager and the bartender would have none of such tomfoolery. They refused me permission to paint the face. Still, the idea haunted me, and in my last night in Central City, I persuaded the bellboy Jimmy Libby to give me a hand.

After midnight, when the coast was clear, we slipped down there. Jimmy held a candle for me and I painted as fast as I could. Yet it was 3 AM when I finished. By the dawn's early light I lit out for Denver.[15]

According to another historical account, the reality of *The Face* and its inception was somewhat different from the artist's version. Davis had had a furious argument that day with Anne Evans, the director of the restoration project. His grimly realistic depictions of gunslingers, gamblers, ladies of the night, and raggedy miners clashed with her vision of the Opera House Association's uplifting mission. Evans, granddaughter of former Colorado territorial governor John Evans, reigned as a "duchess" of Denver society. She insisted that Davis remove the gritty detail in his paintings, and a furious argument ensued. Whether she actually fired him or he quit is unclear, but the bellboy (or busboy, according to the version of the story told by Denver attorney Fred Mazzulla) told Davis, "You're finished here, why not give them something to remember you by?"[16]

While his young accessory sanded off the floor varnish with a brick, the artist fortified himself with rum. This seems apropos, as the 1887 ballad he cited as inspiration, "The Face upon the Floor" by Franco-American poet Hugh Antoine d'Arcy, focused on a heartbroken artist ruined by drink. Once properly lubricated, Davis painted the famous face through the wee hours of the night before making his escape back to Denver. Though it would not be confirmed until his death, rumor had it that the face belonged to his beloved wife, Nita.

Despite the unpleasant break between Davis and Miss Evans, the painting became a hit. The hotel management loved the work and promoted it as a featured attraction in what is now called the Face Bar. Yet Herndon later claimed that after painting *The Face*, he was oblivious to its growing legend.[17] Historian Robert L. Brown records that when he learned that the Teller House was charging an admission fee to see the famous face, an irate Davis went to Central City to sign his work. But to sustain the romance and mystery surrounding the painting, the hotel management removed his signature as soon as he left the building.[18]

Davis's claim that he was unaware of the painting's reputation until the mid-1940s cannot be true. In Davis's papers at the Denver Public Library is a May 26, 1938, letter of recommendation written for the artist by Colorado governor Teller Ammons, complete with the official state seal, crediting Davis's floor painting as "one of the contributing factors in the revival of the summer theatre in Central City."[19] Davis knew exactly how *The Face on the Floor* had been received and the legend that grew up around it. Yet he claimed publicly to be oblivious to the fame of his *Face*. Such self-effacement was characteristic of Herndon Davis.

In 1937, Davis headed for Puerto Rico, where he worked as art director for a newspaper in San Juan, *El Imparcial*. Davis barely escaped unscathed when the offices of the newspaper were bombed by Puerto Rican nationalists who objected to the paper's editorial policies.[20] By February 1938 Davis was back in Denver, exhibiting his *Puerto Rican*

Sketches in Gouache in the Denver Art Museum's now demolished Chappell House at 1300 Logan Street.[21] During this period he also accepted out-of-town work for the City of Carlsbad, New Mexico, the Potash Company of America, and Colorado Fuel and Iron Company at Pueblo.[22]

Davis spent many of his remaining years in Denver working as an illustrator for both the *Rocky Mountain News* and the *Denver Post*. Sometimes he worked for both at once, surely a stressful task since the two papers competed bitterly. Back at home in western environs, Davis painted unique area buildings significant to local and regional history. In 1940–41 he published a prolific series of watercolor renderings of Colorado landmarks called *Survivors of Yesteryear* each week in the Sunday *News*. Journalist Joseph Emerson Smith added narratives for each illustration. Some portrayed architectural landmarks, such as Denver's Richthofen Castle, the Navarre Building, the Windsor Hotel, and the Tabor Grand Opera House. Davis also favored more modest structures with his brush; works like *Littleton Mill* showed the patina of time on a humble edifice of brick and native stone. That now-gone landmark was Richard Little's Rough and Ready Mill, the pioneer industry in what is now Littleton. The brothel of Mattie Silks at 1942 Market Street, which she bought from rival madame Jennie Rogers, was granted its own quiet dignity in Davis's rendering. He treated each building with respect and affection, whether they were the palaces of the rich, the hotels and shops of the common man, or the skeleton of a destroyed building, as in the wistful *Ruins of "Summer White House" Mt. Falcon*, which portrayed the crumbling red brick foundations of John Brisben Walker's unfinished building in Jefferson County, which he intended as a seasonal residence for American presidents. That dream went up in smoke when the would-be western White House burned to the ground. In 1941 an exhibition of these works, dubbed the *Yesteryear Paintings*, was held at the University of Denver. Once again, Davis's newspaper illustrations were recognized as fine art and displayed as such in a gallery setting.[23]

James Quigg Newton, elected mayor of Denver in 1947, was among the many fans of Herndon Davis. He bought the original paintings from the *News* and donated them to the Western History Department of the Denver Public Library. In that wonderful haven of history, Davis's work is often used by and available to one and all to this day.

By all accounts, Davis was very much at home in downtown Denver, including in some seedier locales of the city. He had familiar alley shortcuts to many downtown saloons and often swapped portrait work for bar tabs. Davis painted the likeness of the Keg Buffet owner, A. B. Wade, on a barstool, fulfilling Wade's request so that everyone could "sit on his face."[24] Davis found ready company with a group of "old characters in the Denver newspaper business" who would meet in Wes Hamilton's jewelry store studio, located in the University Building at 16th and Champa Streets downtown. According to author James W. Nikl's account, "When Davis needed money, Hamilton helped him out. In return, Hamilton accumulated a collection of art works that are more than just of monetary value."[25] Davis painted a portrait of Hamilton's deceased father from a photograph that was so vivid as to itself resemble a color photo. "Occasionally Davis would get short of money and would draw up a few sketches or paintings and would sell them for only a dollar or two," wrote Nikl. "A good artist but a poor businessman, he seemed indifferent to success. He worked when he wished and refused when not in the mood. He would work at times with only a hope of selling something."[26] Davis confirmed his profound indifference to money in a 1946 interview with journalist William Barker: "Like most artists, I have no interest in figures—other than those of human beings."[27]

Davis fancied painting murals and left many in and around Denver. From 1937 to 1946, he frequented the bar in Larimer Street's Windsor Hotel (now demolished), painting portraits of the people and the times. The Windsor fell into decay and was razed in 1960. But Herndon's "Portrait Panel" was rescued and transferred by preservationist-developer Dana Crawford to the nearby Oxford Hotel, where it now looks out on the Oxford's Sage Room. It depicts seven prominent figures in Colorado's history: John F. Campion (Leadville silver miner and president of the Denver Chamber of Commerce in 1898), Eugene Field (editor of the *Denver Tribune*), Henry R. Wolcott (a financier who brought outside capital to Denver), William Byers (founding editor of the *Rocky Mountain News*), Frederick Bonfils (co-owner and publisher of the *Denver Post*), Casimiro Barela (prominent rancher, coauthor of the Colorado Constitution, state senator from Trinidad), and Otto Mears (railroad and road builder in southwestern Colorado).[28]

A Davis mural painted and maintained over a twenty-year period in the 1940s and 1950s at Denver's Gilliam Center for Juvenile Justice at 2844 Downing Street was salvaged from the near-ruins of the 1903 building during a 1988 remodeling. The mural, which had been covered over with two other murals by different artists over the years, portrayed revered Denver Juvenile Court judge Ben Lindsey, surrounded by youths and a sea of faces of notable Americans, including George Washington and Thomas Jefferson.[29]

Davis's friends often asked him to adorn their homes with his work. In addition to the Ritter murals described in the preface, Davis painted several elaborate murals in the basement of Denver attorney and historian Fred Mazzulla's home at 1930 East Eighth Avenue in Denver's Cheesman Park neighborhood. The murals portrayed Colorado and other western notables, including Wild Bill Cody, Mayor Robert W. Speer, Soapy Smith, Horace Tabor and Elizabeth "Baby Doe" Tabor, Gene Fowler, Helen Bonfils, David H. Moffat, John Evans, William Byers, William M. Gilpin, and Bishop Joseph P. Machebeuf, among many others. It is believed these murals were created between 1940 and 1947.[30]

Diane Wunnicke produced a video documentary in 1999 giving an up-close look at the Herndon Davis murals in the elegant southeast Denver home of Chauncey and Vida Ritter, at 170 S. Eudora Street in the Hilltop neighborhood. A number of sports-themed

RITTER MURALS

murals reflected a nostalgic and noble vision of athletic competition, including champion heavyweight boxer Jack Dempsey's famous "Long Count" victory over Gene Tunney at Chicago's Soldier Field in 1927, baseball great Babe Ruth with bat at the ready, football star Earl "Dutch" Clark, and the racing dogs of the Mile High Kennel Club. A bar area in the home's recreation room was painted with an elaborate mural of New York City's Bowery section around the turn of the century. Another wall portrayed a row of elegant "ladies and gentlemen of another time," dressed in Victorian garb, while yet another was organized around a circus theme, complete with clowns, elephants, and daring bareback horse riders.

Diane's documentary includes historic preservation efforts to restore a Davis mural in the card room of the Denver Press Club. Painted in 1945, "allegedly in a trade for food and drink," the mural "is an allegorical Denver newsroom depicting some of the most famous characters in the history of Denver journalism."[31] Historic preservationist Carmen Brea is seen cleaning the mural with a gentle solution of triammonium citrate and distilled water, removing the dulling film left by decades of cigar and cigarette smoke.[32] Fittingly, the room is now known as the Herndon Davis Room.

Davis further indulged his fondness for history with a 1951–52 series for the *Post* entitled *Once upon a Time*, which paired his evocative sketches of places, people, and events from western history with brief text summaries. Subjects ranged from early western history topics, such as "Cortes' Horse Sees a Ghost" and [Spanish explorer Juan de] "Oñate's Caravan," to mythic nineteenth-century Wild West figures like "Uncle Dick" Wootton, Pecos Bill, and Judge Roy Bean. The series was thoughtful and erudite, showing how far Davis had come since his days portraying dancing girls for a living.

Davis applied his talents to an unusual scheme in the 1950s—a plan to design postage stamps for the Republic of Panama featuring the likenesses of all 259 Roman Catholic popes.[33] The plan was financed by well-heeled investors who hoped for a big return by selling the stamps to the world's millions of Catholic stamp collectors. Davis began by painting all of the popes named Pius. But the first run sold only 9,000 stamps, a drop in the bucket compared to the millions investors had hoped to peddle. Davis lost his plum assignment as the scheme went belly-up in 1957.[34]

In summation, Davis is remembered more for his subject matter than for his artistic ability. Among Colorado artists of his time, he is most notable for the historic characters and places he drew and painted. One contemporary artist, Muriel Sibell Wolle (1898–1977), drew and painted hundreds of buildings, many of which are showcased in her classic book, *Stampede the Timberline*, and other smaller, similar works. She was more prolific than Davis but focused only on buildings. Waldo Love (1881–1967) painted habitat backgrounds for the Denver Museum of Natural History, as well as historical portraits and illustrated maps for the Colorado Historical Society. Artist Juan Menchaca (1910–99) did portraits and dioramas for the Colorado History Museum under the auspices of the Works Progress Administration. Menchaca's work is not as prolific or well-known as that of Davis. Both Vance Kirkland (1904–81), probably the best-known and most influential Colorado artist of the twentieth century, and Allen True (1881–1955), the best-known muralist, have been covered in at least one book. Except for an exhibit at the Denver Public Library Western History and Genealogy Department and use of his work in various local publications, Herndon Davis has not received the attention we think he deserves. He was not a great artist or concerned with "fine" art, but he did popular work on popular topics. This may help to explain why art historians have largely ignored him. Yet within the sphere of contemporary artists who focused on documenting Colorado's past, Davis provides the greatest gallery of portraits and places.

Davis received a commission to paint a giant mural for the Smithsonian Institution in 1962, but it was not to be. On November 7, 1962, Davis "collapsed across his drawing board and died of a heart attack . . . in Washington, where he had been at work for nine months."[35] Davis is buried at Fort Logan National Cemetery in Denver. His wife, Juanita (or "Nita"), passed away in 1975, freeing the couple's friends from their pledge to keep her identity as the model of the Teller House face on the barroom floor a secret.[36]

The Face remains the most famous part of Herndon Davis's legacy; its Wild West setting and inherent mystery and romance make it an irresistible symbol for the career of the artist himself. Like *The Face*, Davis has inspired many stories, with various shades of truth and fancy. His renderings of generals, presidents, athletes, and movie stars entertained millions of newspaper readers and art lovers. His loving portrayals of the people, places, and landscapes of the West will continue to illuminate its history and heritage for generations to come.

THE ART OF

HERNDON

DAVIS

WILLIAM "BILLY" ADAMS

PAINTING, History Colorado

William Herbert Adams (1861–1954), better known as Billy Adams, governed Colorado from 1927 until 1933. Born in Blue Mounds, Wisconsin, Adams moved to Alamosa, Colorado, at age seventeen. He gradually climbed the ranks of city and then state government, serving at different times as Alamosa city treasurer, mayor of Alamosa, Conejos County commissioner, state representative, and, beginning in 1888, state senator. He held his seat in the senate for thirty-eight years, before winning election as governor of Colorado in 1926.

Adams was no reformer. His administration was characterized by economy and conservatism. He dealt sternly with a three-month coal strike that started in late 1927, forming a State Law Enforcement Agency under the command of a veteran of the Ludlow Massacre. Eight workers were shot down by Adams's agency between November 1927 and January 1928.

Politics ran in the Adams family. Billy's older brother, Alva Adams, also served as governor of Colorado, from 1887 to 1889, from 1897 to 1899, and in 1905. Billy's nephew, Alva Blanchard Adams, was a US senator from Colorado from 1923 to 1925 and from 1933 to 1941. As a Colorado state senator in 1921, Adams pushed through a bill to create the Alamosa State Normal School in Alamosa, Colorado. The college's name was later changed to Adams State Teachers College to honor Governor Adams. It is now known as Adams State University.

ETHEL BARRYMORE

PEN AND INK DRAWING, 1931, DENVER PUBLIC LIBRARY
WESTERN HISTORY AND GENEALOGY DEPARTMENT.
PUBLISHED NOVEMBER 8, 1931, IN THE SUNDAY *NEW
YORK HERALD TRIBUNE.*

Ethel Barrymore (1879–1959) debuted as a New
York City stage actress in 1894, captivating audiences with her soulful dark eyes and distinctive
voice. Breakthrough roles included working with
English great Henry Irving in *The Bells* (1897)
and *Peter the Great* (1898), as well as in the Clyde
Fitch play *Captain Jinks of the Horse Marines* (1901).
Leading roles in *A Doll's House* (1905), *Mid-Channel*
(1910), and *Trelawney of the Wells* (1911) sealed her
popularity as a star of the American stage. Although
the stage was always her first love, Barrymore also
appeared in film and television, but her screen
stardom never matched that of her brother John
Barrymore. This characteristically intricate Herndon
Davis pen and ink illustration captures Barrymore
in a 1931 revival of *School for Scandal.*

CARLOS BEAUBIEN

WATERCOLOR, 1961, DENVER PUBLIC LIBRARY
WESTERN HISTORY AND GENEALOGY DEPARTMENT

Québécois-born Carlos Beaubien (1800–1864) figures prominently in the history of New Mexico and Colorado. He first came to New Mexico by way of St. Louis with a party of French fur trappers, including fellow pioneers Ceran St. Vrain and Antoine Leroux. Beaubien became a Mexican citizen and a prosperous trader. He acquired interests in what came to be known as the Beaubien-Miranda Land Grant in 1841 and the Sangre de Cristo Land Grant in 1844. Both straddle the border between present-day New Mexico and Colorado. When war came between the United States and Mexico, Beaubien switched allegiance, serving under the US New Mexico governor Charles Bent as a territorial supreme court justice. When the Taos Revolt erupted in January 1847, Beaubien's son Narciso was killed, along with Governor Bent and many others. Beaubien presided over the trials of the accused killers, earning a reputation for meting out stern justice.

FREDERICK BONFILS

PAINTING, HISTORY COLORADO

Frederick Gilmer Bonfils (1860–1933) turned the *Denver Post* into one of the largest—and least respected—newspapers in the United States. Born in Troy, Missouri, Bonfils entered the United States Military Academy in 1878 but resigned in 1881 to pursue land speculation in Kansas, Oklahoma, and Texas. Bonfils met future partner Harry Heye Tammen at the Windsor Hotel in Denver, where Tammen tended bar. They bought the *Post* in 1895 and made it a financial success by turning to sensational yellow journalism. Their often slanderous attacks also made them their share of enemies. In 1899 Bonfils and Tammen were shot in the *Post* offices by an angry lawyer; the following year they were hospitalized after being horse-whipped by another enemy. Bonfils was known to threaten merchants with exposés if they did not advertise in his newspaper. In 1922 the *Post* questioned sweetheart oil leases granted by the federal government to the Sinclair Oil Company but cut short its inquiry after Sinclair paid off Bonfils and Tammen. At the time of Bonfils's death from encephalitis in 1933, he was pursuing a libel lawsuit against the *Post*'s rival and competitor, the *Rocky Mountain News*. His two daughters, May and Helen, strove to improve the family reputation with extensive philanthropic activities.

HELEN BONFILS

Helen Bonfils (1889–1972) was a prominent Colorado philanthropist and the daughter of Frederick Gilmer Bonfils, co-founder and co-publisher of the *Denver Post*. Her first love was not journalism but theater, and she became an actress at Elitch Gardens Theatre in Denver, which she also supported financially. Later, she established a swanky apartment in New York City and became a Broadway producer. Her philanthropy and love of theater led to the estab-lishment of the Bonfils Memorial Theater and the Denver Center for the Performing Arts. She also founded the Belle Bonfils Blood Bank and built Holy Ghost Church in downtown Denver. She co-owned the *Denver Post* after her father's death in 1933 until her own death in 1972.

MARGARET "MOLLY" BROWN

PAINTING, HISTORY COLORADO

Margaret "Molly" Tobin Brown (1867–1932) was a socialite and philanthropist who became one of Colorado's most famous women after surviving the 1912 sinking of the *Titanic*. Margaret Tobin was born in Hannibal, Missouri. She came to Leadville, Colorado, in 1886 and married James Joseph "J.J." Brown, manager and part owner of a mine. The Browns became very wealthy when J.J.'s engineering work for the Ibex Mining Company proved critical to the production of a major gold ore vein at the "Little Jonny" Mine. J.J. was awarded shares of stock and a seat on the board, allowing the Browns to move to Denver in 1894. They bought a substantial home on Denver's Capitol Hill at 1340 Pennsylvania Street, and Margaret entered the city's social life, with mixed success. She entertained lavishly and starred in Catholic circles, where she became a benefactor of Saint Joseph Hospital and Immaculate Conception Cathedral, but she was reportedly snubbed by the elite of Denver's social hierarchy, who felt she lacked education and couth. Besides, she was Irish and Catholic.

Following her widely reported heroics helping others escape the sinking *Titanic,* she gained international fame and greater social respectability in Denver. Margaret used her fame and wealth to pursue many civic, charitable, and activist endeavors. She worked with Judge Ben Lindsey to help destitute children and to establish the country's first juvenile court. Margaret ran for the US Senate in 1909 and 1914 and organized an international women's rights conference in Rhode Island in July 1914. During World War I, she served with the American Committee for Devastated France, tending to wounded American and French soldiers. Margaret separated from her husband, J.J. Brown, and became involved in legal battles with her children over his estate after he died in 1922. She reconciled with her children, however, before her passing in 1932. The Molly Brown House in Denver has been restored as a popular tourist attraction that tells her story.

WILLIAM N. BYERS

PAINTING, HISTORY COLORADO

William Newton Byers (1831–1903), a surveyor, editor, and businessman, helped found Omaha, Nebraska, and brought the Colorado Territory its first newspaper. Born in Ohio, Byers moved with his parents to the fledging town of Omaha in 1854. He created Omaha's first official plat and served on the city council and in the first Nebraska Territorial Legislature. In 1859 he followed the gold rush to Denver, hauling the printing presses of the defunct *Bellevue Gazette* with him in an oxcart. Byers and his associates published the first issue of the *Rocky Mountain News* on April 23, 1859, beating their nearest competitor to print by twenty minutes to become the first newspaper published in Colorado. Byers was a "booster," who used the platform of the *News* to trumpet the unlimited opportunities in what was then still western Kansas Territory. Byers explained his motives for establishing the *News* in its first issue: "We have done this because we wished to collect and send forth reliable information, because we wished to help mold and organize the new population, and because we thought it would pay."

Byers sold the *Rocky Mountain News* in 1878, focusing on other business interests and remaining an ardent Colorado booster until his death in 1903. The *News* lasted until 2009, at which time it was not only the state's oldest newspaper but possibly the longest continuously operating business in Colorado. Byers, Colorado's greatest promoter, sometimes stretched the truth, claiming, for instance, that steamboat service to Denver existed. His energetic interest in all aspects of Denver and Colorado and his tireless newspaper promotion of Denver did much to transform a little village in the middle of nowhere into the Rocky Mountain metropolis.

MOTHER CABRINI

PAINTING, HISTORY COLORADO

Saint Frances Xavier Cabrini (1850–1917), also known as Mother Cabrini, was an Italian nun who founded the Missionary Sisters of the Sacred Heart, a Catholic organization to aid Italian immigrants to the United States. Cabrini became the first US citizen to be canonized by the Roman Catholic Church.

Born two months premature in the Lombard Province of Lodi, she remained in delicate health throughout her life. Her good works as founder of the Missionary Sisters brought Mother Cabrini to the attention of Pope Leo XIII. Cabrini sought the pope's approval to establish missions in China. Instead, he directed her to go to the United States and help the masses of impoverished Italian immigrants emigrating there in the late nineteenth century.

Cabrini arrived in New York City on March 31, 1889, along with six other sisters. There she founded an orphanage, the first of sixty-seven such institutions she fostered in New York, Chicago, Des Plaines, Seattle, New Orleans, Denver, Golden, Los Angeles, and Philadelphia, as well as throughout South America and Europe. While visiting Italian immigrants in the Colorado mining districts, Mother Cabrini became drawn to a property on the southeast slope of Lookout Mountain. In 1910 she purchased this property near Golden as a summer camp for the children of the Queen of Heaven Orphanage in Denver and established a farm there. The only water on the property came from a small pond, and water needed for drinking and cooking had to be brought up to the camp from the stream at the bottom of Mt. Vernon Canyon, prompting complaints to Mother Cabrini from the sisters who managed the camp. Cabrini instructed the sisters to "lift that rock over there and start to dig. You will find water fresh enough to drink and clean enough to wash with." They did as she directed and found a freshwater spring that has never since stopped running. That hilltop spring has become a shrine, visited each year by thousands of pilgrims who believe the water has healing qualities.

MARTHA "CALAMITY JANE" CANARY

PEN DRAWING, 1961, DENVER PUBLIC LIBRARY
WESTERN HISTORY AND GENEALOGY DEPARTMENT

Calamity Jane (1852–1903), a legendary frontierswoman and professional scout who defied expectations for women with her daring exploits, garnered a reputation for kindness and compassion. She was born Martha Jane Canary in Princeton, Missouri. Details of her life are sketchy, as most information about her comes from an autobiographical publicity pamphlet. Jane made unconfirmed claims of having fought Indians in Wyoming and of being a longtime companion of Wild Bill Hickok, with whom she arrived at Deadwood, South Dakota, in 1876. She won goodwill there by rescuing a stagecoach from Indian attack and by nursing victims of a smallpox outbreak. Suffering from depression and alcoholism in later years, Jane nonetheless traded on her fame by joining Buffalo Bill's Wild West Show as a storyteller in 1893 and participating in the 1901 Pan-American Exposition. She died in 1903 after a bout of heavy drinking in Terry, South Dakota.

HERNDON DAVIS
DEADWOOD

RALPH L. CARR

PAINTING, HISTORY COLORADO

Ralph Lawrence Carr (1887–1950) was a lawyer, editor, and politician who served as the twenty-ninth governor of Colorado. Born in Rosita, Colorado, in Custer County, he grew up in Cripple Creek and earned his BA and his law degree at the University of Colorado at Boulder. Carr worked as a newspaper editor and as a lawyer, specializing in irrigation law and helping Colorado delegations negotiate interstate river compacts during the 1920s. He was elected governor in 1938 and again in 1940. A fiscally conservative Republican, Carr opposed the New Deal policies of President Franklin D. Roosevelt but supported Roosevelt's foreign policy. When FDR's War Relocation Authority interred Japanese Americans from the West Coast at Camp Amache near Granada, Colorado, Carr urged Coloradans to accept the evacuees. Defending the rights of the displaced Japanese Americans, Carr said: "If you harm them, you must harm me. I was brought up in a small town where I knew the shame and dishonor of race hatred. I grew to despise it because it threatened the happiness of you and you and you." Carr's stance for racial tolerance undid his political career. He narrowly lost his 1942 bid for a US Senate seat to incumbent Democrat Edwin C. Johnson, who accused Carr of coddling "Japs." Carr is warmly remembered by Colorado's Japanese American community, which honored him in 1976 with a bust in Sakura Square at 19th and Larimer Streets in Denver. In 2013 the Ralph L. Carr Colorado Judicial Center opened in downtown Denver's Civic Center, commemorating the late governor whose courageous defense of a hated minority cost him his political career.

CHRISTOPHER "KIT" CARSON

PEN AND INK ON PAPER, DENVER PUBLIC LIBRARY WESTERN HISTORY AND GENEALOGY DEPARTMENT

Christopher Houston "Kit" Carson (1809–68) was a western frontiersman, scout, and Indian fighter. Born in Missouri, Carson went west as a trapper, roaming to California and through the Rocky Mountains. Carson served the expeditions of John C. Frémont as a guide through much of California, Oregon, and the Great Basin area and gained fame from Frémont's accounts of their travels. Carson

served the US government as a courier and scout during the Mexican-American War of 1846–48, as an Indian agent in the 1850s, and as a colonel leading New Mexican volunteers during the Civil War. Carson led armies to pacify the Navajo, Apache, Kiowa, and Comanche Indians. His scorched earth campaign and slaughtering of many Navajo (Diné) made him notorious to many.

SAUL CASTON

PENCIL, 1961, Denver Public Library Western History and Genealogy Department

Caston (1901–70) served as conductor and music director of the Denver Symphony Orchestra from 1945 to 1964. He grew the orchestra's reach and popularity by bringing music into local schools, touring, offering family discounts to Denver residents, and performing outdoors at Red Rocks Amphitheatre near Morrison. A 1951 article in *Time* magazine credited Caston with the orchestra's success and with giving it a national profile. Davis drew this portrait for the *History of Red Rocks Park and Theater* by Nolie Mumey.

GEORGE CATLIN

WATERCOLOR AND GOUACHE PAINTING, CA. 1951,
DENVER PUBLIC LIBRARY WESTERN HISTORY AND
GENEALOGY DEPARTMENT

Painter George Catlin (1796–1872) from Wilkes-
Barre, Pennsylvania, made it his mission to record
the appearance and customs of the Native American
tribes, whom he believed were a vanishing people.
Between 1830 and 1836, Catlin traveled thousands
of miles along the trail of the Lewis and Clark expedition, visiting and painting members of fifty tribes
living west of the Mississippi River, from Oklahoma
to present-day North Dakota. He later toured the
world with his *Indian Gallery* of more than 500 portraits. The collection, which constitutes a priceless
record of native cultures at a crucial crossroads of
American history, now resides in the Smithsonian.
This piece was created for Davis's *Once upon a Time*
series for the *Denver Post*, which paired his evocative renderings of people, places, and events from
western history with brief written narratives.

CHIPETA

PAINTING, HISTORY COLORADO

Chipeta (ca. 1843–1924), which means "White Singing Bird" in the Ute language, became the second wife of Chief Ouray of the Uncompahgre Ute tribe. When she was a baby, a band of Tabeguache Utes found the infant Chipeta crawling in the ruins of a Kiowa Apache village. The Utes raised her near what is now Conejos, Colorado. She became caretaker to Chief Ouray's children after his wife died and soon became his new wife. She aided her husband's diplomacy, counseling with visiting chiefs and federal government functionaries. She continued in a leadership role after her husband's death in 1880, but government promises were revoked and Chipeta left Ute lands in Colorado, along with the rest of the tribe, for a reservation in Utah. On the Uintah Reservation, the Utes faced a harsh climate that made their traditional means of farming impossible. Even in the Utah desert, miners and government agents tricked the Utes and stole their land, whittling down their reservation. Chipeta and her fellow Utes strove to survive on government rations.

A *Rocky Mountain News* reporter first labeled Chipeta "Queen of the Utes" in a facetious and derogatory tone. But when Denver journalist Eugene Field wrote a poem dedicated to Chipeta for her role in saving whites held hostage by Utes after the Meeker Massacre, the public embraced and idealized her for her wisdom, beauty, and grace, making her as famous as Ouray. Today, her name graces streets and places all over Colorado and Utah. After Chipeta died in 1924, the city of Montrose, Colorado, insisted she be exhumed from her humble grave in Utah and buried with pomp and circumstance in Montrose, where she continues to rest in her ancestral homeland. Her grave is a major attraction of the Ute Indian Museum and park.

WILLIAM F. "BUFFALO BILL" CODY

PENCIL WITH WATERCOLOR ACCENTS, 1961, DENVER PUBLIC LIBRARY WESTERN HISTORY AND GENEALOGY DEPARTMENT

William "Buffalo Bill" Cody (1846–1917), a US Army scout, buffalo hunter, showman, and prototypical western hero, was born in the Iowa Territory. He lived several years in Canada as a child before his family moved to the Kansas Territory. Cody served in the US Army during the Civil War and in subsequent Indian campaigns. In 1872 he began his show business career at age twenty-six in a show called "Scouts of the Prairie." The following year, Cody organized his own troupe, the Buffalo Bill Combination, including fellow western legends Texas Jack and "Wild Bill" Hickok. In 1882 he began Buffalo Bill's Wild West Show, which made him famous around the world. Buffalo Bill's Wild West Show was a grand spectacle, designed to both educate and entertain. It included a cast of hundreds of real cowboys and cowgirls, recruited from western ranches, demonstrating bronco riding and roping. The show visited England in 1887 as the main American contribution to Queen Victoria's Golden Jubilee celebration, becoming a giant hit with the British public and with the queen herself.

Buffalo Bill included Native Americans in his show, giving his former adversaries an opportunity to leave the reservation and represent their culture to curious audiences. Buffalo Bill stated in 1885 that "the defeat of Custer was not a massacre. The Indians were being pursued by skilled fighters with orders to kill. For centuries they had been hounded from the Atlantic to the Pacific and back again. They had their wives and little ones to protect and they were fighting for their existence." Davis prepared this illustration for the book *History of Red Rocks Park and Theater* by Nolie Mumey.

BETTE DAVIS

PEN AND INK DRAWING, 1935, DENVER PUBLIC LIBRARY
WESTERN HISTORY AND GENEALOGY DEPARTMENT.
PUBLISHED IN THE *WASHINGTON POST*, JUNE 9, 1935.

Ruth Elizabeth Davis (1908–89), known to the world as movie star Bette Davis, was born in Lowell, Massachusetts, in 1908. She broke into show business by starring in the off-Broadway play *The Earth Between* (1923), and her Broadway debut came in 1929's *Broken Dishes*. In 1932 she signed a seven-year deal with Warner Brothers Pictures and became a star after her appearance in *The Man Who Played God* (1932). In 1934 she scored a smash in *Of Human Bondage* while on loan from Warner's to RKO. Davis won Oscars for her work in *Dangerous* (1935) and *Jezebel* (1938). She continued acting into the 1970s. This Herndon Davis portrait, done in his distinctive pen and ink cross-hatching style, was published amid publicity for Bette's 1935 film *The Girl from Tenth Avenue*.

12 yrs

1914

HERNDON DAVIS SELF-PORTRAIT

CHARCOAL ON PAPER, 1914, DENVER PUBLIC LIBRARY
WESTERN HISTORY AND GENEALOGY DEPARTMENT

Davis showed remarkable sensitivity and talent in
this self-portrait, created at age twelve.

HERNDON DAVIS SELF-PORTRAIT 2

This later self-portrait looks as though it were done in haste by an artist who is comfortable in his own skin but does not take himself too seriously.

JACK DEMPSEY

PAINTING, HISTORY COLORADO

Boxer William Harrison "Jack" Dempsey (1895–1983), nick-named "the Manassa Mauler," held the World Heavyweight Championship from 1919 to 1926. His aggressive style and spectacular punching power made him one of the most popular professional athletes of his day. Raised in a poor family in Manassa, Colorado, as William Harrison Dempsey, he grew up in Colorado, West Virginia, and Utah. His ancestry was part Irish and part Cherokee and included a Jewish paternal great-great-grandmother, and his family members were Mormon converts. Dempsey left home at age sixteen to pursue a career in boxing. The young Dempsey visited saloons in search of a fight, saying "I can't sing and I can't dance, but I can lick any SOB in the house." He first fought as Jack Dempsey in 1914, in tribute to an earlier middleweight boxer known as Jack "Nonpareil" Dempsey. He defended his heavyweight title five times before losing it to challenger Gene Tunney in 1926. Dempsey lost a controversial rematch in 1927 and retired from boxing. He went on to open a restaurant in New York City and to try his hand at acting, appearing in a handful of films including *The Prizefighter and the Lady* (1933) and *Sweet Surrender* (1935).

JAMES W. DENVER

PAINTING, HISTORY COLORADO

A politician, soldier, and lawyer, James William Denver (1817–92) was born in Winchester, Virginia, educated in Ohio, and admitted to the Ohio bar in 1844. In 1847 Denver volunteered for the Mexican-American War and received a commission as captain of the 12th US Volunteer Infantry, serving under General Winfield Scott. After the war, in 1850, Denver traveled to California, where he had a colorful career as a trader and a duelist, killing newspaper editor Edward Gilbert in a duel on August 2, 1852. Later that year he turned to politics, winning a seat in the California State Senate, which led to an appointment as secretary of state of California and a term in the US Congress as a representative from California from 1855 to 1857. In April 1857, President James Buchanan appointed Denver commissioner of Indian affairs and in December of that year appointed him territorial governor of Kansas. The day Denver assumed office, residents voted on a constitution that would have opened the territory to slavery. The pro-slavery constitution passed by a large margin, but it was later discovered that thousands of votes were cast fraudulently by pro-slavery Missourians who had crossed the border to tilt the election.

Much of present-day eastern Colorado lay in Kansas Territory in the late 1850s. While Denver served as territorial governor, land speculator William Larimer Jr. platted the town site of "Denver City" along the South Platte River around its confluence with Cherry Creek in Arapaho County in western Kansas Territory. Larimer chose the name to flatter the governor and to encourage him to select his namesake as the county seat of Arapaho County.

Denver left his position as territorial governor in November 1858 and was reappointed commissioner of Indian affairs, serving in that post until March 1859. Shortly after the beginning of the Civil War, President Abraham Lincoln commissioned Denver as a brigadier general in the Union Army. He commanded all federal troops in Kansas from December 1861 until April 1862, when he transferred to the District of West Tennessee. He led his troops with distinction at the Siege of Corinth under General William T. Sherman and served in the Vicksburg campaign before his resignation from the army on March 5, 1863. Denver went on to practice law in Washington, DC, and Wilmington, Ohio. He was active in Democratic Party politics in the 1870s and 1880s, even mentioned as a possible Democratic presidential nominee in 1876 and 1884. The retired general visited his namesake city in 1875 and 1882 but reportedly complained about the lack of affection the city showed him. Denver died in Washington, DC, in 1892.

ELEANOR DUMONT (MADAME MOUSTACHE)

PENCIL ON PAPER, 1961, DENVER PUBLIC LIBRARY WESTERN HISTORY AND GENEALOGY DEPARTMENT

Madame Moustache was the pseudonym of Eleanor Dumont (1839–79), a celebrated frontier gambler and card dealer from France who came to the American West with the California Gold Rush as a young woman. She made a living from twenty-one and other casino games. Dumont opened a gambling parlor known as Vingt-et-un in Nevada City, California. Her good looks, charismatic personality, and the novelty of a female dealer drew a steady stream of customers. She partnered with experienced gambler Dave Tobin as proprietor of Dumont's Place, which did a booming business until the gold rush crashed in Nevada City. Dumont left for new opportunities. She parlayed her success at cards into a ranch at Carson City,

Nevada, where she fell in love with Jack McKnight who conned her out of her fortune, compelling her to resume her life as a roving gambler. As her beauty began to fade with age, a dark line of hair began to grow on her lip and became the basis of her new moniker: Madame Moustache. Dumont's unblemished reputation for dealing fair meant she still drew crowds. She became involved in prostitution in the 1860s, running a brothel and parading her girls around the town in carriages during the day to entice potential customers. One night while gambling in Bodie, California, Dumont hit a patch of bad luck and suddenly owed a lot of money. That night, September 8, 1879, she was found dead of suicide from an overdose of morphine.

ESPINOSA BROTHERS' HEADS

PEN AND WATERCOLOR, HISTORY COLORADO

Felipe Espinosa, aided by his brother, Vivian, and later a nephew, José, terrorized Anglo settlers in southern Colorado in the 1860s. Resentful of incursions into Spanish-speaking communities, of losses in the Mexican-American War, and, according to some sources, of the rape of their sister by white men, the Espinosas killed and mutilated an esti-

mated thirty-two gringos. A protracted manhunt proved fruitless until famed hunter Tom Tobin caught up with the Espinosas in 1864. Davis's painting portrays the moment when Tobin presented Volunteer Commander Samuel Forster Tappan and his wife with the heads of the slain outlaws at Fort Garland.

ANNE EVANS

PAINTING, History Colorado

The daughter of John Evans, Colorado's second territorial governor, and his wife, Margaret Patten Gray Evans, Anne Evans (1871–1941) was born in London and educated in Paris, Berlin, and New York. She never married and devoted much of her time to supporting the arts and other civic and cultural causes for which she cared passionately. An early admirer and collector of Native American art, Evans eventually donated her collection to establish the Native American Art Department at the Denver Art Museum. This was the first major museum to have a separate Native Arts Department and to realize that the "curiosities of the savages" were often of high artistic merit. The hard-driving Evans contributed to Denver's cultural and civic development in many ways. Projects she oversaw, initiated, or influenced included the Denver Art Museum, the Denver Public Library, restoration of the Central City Opera House and creation of its Summer Festival, the expansion of the Denver University Art and Theatre Departments, the founding of Kent Country Day School, and Mayor Speer's creation of the Civic Center. Evans sat on the board of the influential Denver Art Commission, which sought to beautify the city, and served as vice president of the Evans Investment Company. She hired Herndon Davis to help with Central City projects. She once said, "You have to get angry with people sometimes or they'll think they can run over you, especially if you're a woman." She added that she achieved a lot by letting others, especially men, take credit for her accomplishments.

JOHN EVANS

Physician, politician, railroader, and businessman, John Evans (1814–97) served as governor of the Territory of Colorado. Born in Waynesville, Ohio, Evans studied in Philadelphia and Cincinnati before beginning his medical practice in Attica, Indiana. Evans counted Abraham Lincoln as a friend and helped found the Illinois Republican Party. Lincoln appointed Evans the second governor of the Territory of Colorado in 1862. In 1864, Evans founded Colorado's first institution of higher learning, the Colorado Seminary, which became the University of Denver. In August 1864, Evans put his friend the reverend John M. Chivington in command of the Third Colorado Regiment to guard against Indian attacks. On November 29, Chivington ordered an attack on Black Kettle's peaceful camp of Arapaho and Cheyenne at Sand Creek. An estimated 165 men, women, and children were killed and mutilated. Governor Evans decorated Chivington and his men for their "valor in subduing the savages," but the massacre soon attracted congressional investigation, condemnation, and censure. Evans was compelled to testify before the US Congress and was subsequently accused of a cover-up. President Andrew Johnson asked him to resign as governor in July 1865. Nonetheless, Evans remained popular with many Colorado settlers for his perceived "toughness" against the natives. Evans continued to serve as chairman of the Denver Seminary Board of Trustees and to play a role in developing Denver railroads, streetcars, and real estate until his death. Evanston, Illinois, Evans, Colorado and Mount Evans, Colorado all bear his name.

THE FACE ON THE BARROOM FLOOR

PAINTING, 1936. THE TELLER HOUSE BAR IN CENTRAL CITY CHERISHES THE ORIGINAL; COPIES ARE IN DENVER PUBLIC LIBRARY WESTERN HISTORY AND GENEALOGY DEPARTMENT

In 1936, Herndon Davis accepted a commission from the Central City Opera House Association (CCOHA) to create a series of paintings and sketches of the mountain town, which CCOHA was reviving as an opera center and tourist attraction. Arts maven and CCOHA head Anne Evans took issue with the gritty realism of some of Davis's work, and a vigorous disagreement ensued. Whether Davis quit or was fired is not clear, but before he returned to Denver he left a remarkable calling card. Inspired by Hugh Antoine d'Arcy's famous poem "The Face upon the Floor," Davis worked all night painting this alluring feminine likeness on the floor of the Teller House Bar. When he departed from Central City at dawn's light, he left behind what would become the most famous and beloved work of his career. *The Face* was a hit with hotel management and visitors alike. Though not confirmed until after his death, the model for the famous *Face* was Davis's wife, Edna Juanita (Cotter) Davis, known to friends as "Nita."

DOUGLAS FAIRBANKS

PAINTING, HISTORY COLORADO

Actor, screenwriter, director, and producer Douglas Fairbanks Sr. (1883–1939) hailed from Denver, Colorado. Born Douglas Elton Thomas Ullman, Fairbanks took to acting as a child, performing in summer stock at the Elitch Gardens Theatre. He attended Denver's East High School, which once expelled him for dressing up the campus statues as a prank. He left during his senior year to move to New York City, after being discovered by the British actor Frederick Warde when he passed through Denver with his acting troupe.

Fairbanks became a national star in his teens. He made his Broadway debut in 1902, but his biggest impact was as a movie star. By the time he retired from acting in the 1930s, he had fifty total screen credits. Before the 1920s, Fairbanks starred mostly in comedies, but he is best remembered for a string of wildly popular swashbuckling adventures with elaborate, impressive sets and costumes, such as *The Three Musketeers* (1921), *Douglas Fairbanks as Robin Hood* (1922), *The Thief of Bagdad* (1924), *The Black Pirate* (1926, the first full-length Technicolor film), and *The Gaucho* (1927). Fairbanks's enthusiasm for acting and his popularity with audiences declined with the advent of "talkies." Audiences were turned off by his collaboration with his wife, Mary Pickford, in Shakespeare's *The Taming of the Shrew* (1929), and his last role of note was in the British production *The Private Life of Don Juan* (1934). He, Pickford, and their close friend Charlie Chaplin created United Artists in 1919 and made it one of Hollywood's most successful movie makers.

EUGENE FIELD

PAINTING, HISTORY COLORADO

Writer and journalist Eugene Field Sr. (1850–95) is best known for his humorous essays and poetry for children. He was born in St. Louis, Missouri, where his boyhood home has been preserved as the Eugene Field House and St. Louis Toy Museum. Field's father, attorney Roswell Martin Field, was famous for representing Dred Scott, the slave who sued for his freedom in a case sometimes called "the lawsuit that started the Civil War." The younger Field went to work as a journalist for the *St. Joseph Gazette* in Saint Joseph, Missouri, in 1875. He soon became known for his humorous articles written in a gossipy style, many of which were reprinted by other newspapers around the country. As his star climbed, Field worked for larger papers, including St. Louis's *Morning Journal* and *Times-Journal*. After a stint as managing editor of the *Kansas City Times*, he worked for two years as editor of the *Denver Tribune*. While in Denver, he lived in the Eugene Field Cottage, now a designated landmark relocated to Denver's Washington Park. In 1883 Field moved east to write for the *Chicago Daily News*. His popular Sharps and Flats column covered arts and literature and trumpeted the merits of the Windy City. Field published over a dozen volumes of light-hearted poetry for children, most famously *Wynken, Blynken, and Nod* and *The Gingham Dog and the Calico Cat*. He also penned a number of short stories, including "The Holy Cross" and "Daniel and the Devil." Field died in Chicago of a heart attack at age forty-five.

MARY GARDEN

PENCIL ON PAPER WITH WATERCOLOR ACCENT, 1961,
DENVER PUBLIC LIBRARY WESTERN HISTORY AND
GENEALOGY DEPARTMENT

Contemporaries hailed Scottish American operatic soprano Mary Garden (1874–1967) as "the
Sarah Bernhardt of opera." Her star first rose in
Paris when she became leading soprano at the
Opéra-Comique. She was featured in several
world premieres, including Mélisande in Claude
Debussy's *Pelléas et Mélisande* (1902) and the title role
in Jules Massenet's opera *Chérubin* (1905). In 1907
she joined Oscar Hammerstein's Manhattan Opera
House in New York City, which led to national
fame and recognition. In 1922 she became director
of the Chicago Civic Opera. She also appeared in
two silent films made by Samuel Goldwyn. Garden
sang at the Red Rocks Amphitheatre in 1911 and
declared it "acoustically perfect." This illustration
was created for *History of Red Rocks Park and Theater*
by Nolie Mumey.

WILLIAM GILPIN

GOUACHE ON PAPER, DENVER PUBLIC LIBRARY
WESTERN HISTORY AND GENEALOGY DEPARTMENT

William Gilpin (1813–94) is best remembered as the first territorial governor of Colorado. He accompanied John C. Frémont on his second expedition through the West and helped create the first territorial government of the Oregon Territory. President Abraham Lincoln appointed Gilpin the first governor of the Colorado Territory, but his unauthorized expenditures to finance Colorado's Civil War mobilization brought down his administration. Forced to resign in 1862, he stayed in Denver working as a land speculator, railroad promoter, and booster.

JOHN H. GREGORY

PAINTING, HISTORY COLORADO

Georgia native John Hamilton Gregory discovered the first gold lode in Colorado, between the present sites of Blackhawk and Central City. Gregory joined a party of three other Georgians at Auraria and proceeded to make the historic strike in North Clear Creek on May 6, 1859. Climbing to the source of a promising wash, Gregory filled his pan with dirt, panned it out, and found four dollars' worth of gold. William Byers, editor of the *Rocky Mountain News*, arrived at Gregory Diggings on May 19 and reported that when he struck it rich, Gregory exclaimed, "My wife will be a lady, and my children will be educated."

The *New York Tribune*'s editor, Horace Greeley, was among the legion of eastern journalists who descended on Gregory Diggings to report on the frenzy. A new rush commenced, and within weeks as many as 5,000 men were crowding the ravines in the vicinity of Gregory's find, trying to strike it rich. Gregory sold his two claims for the relatively modest sum of $21,000 in the summer of 1859. He prospected for others for a time, but soon afterward he left the district. As historian Elliott West wrote, "Gregory, who had a reputation for low energy and spotty attention, reportedly was so addled by his good luck that he sold his claim within weeks. After drifting around the country for a couple of years, he checked out of an Illinois hotel and disappeared from the record." This Herndon Davis portrait is the only known image of John Gregory, who vanished shortly after making Colorado's first great gold discovery.

EMILY GRIFFITH

PAINTING, HISTORY COLORADO

Beloved Denver educator Emily Griffith (1868–1947) improved the lives of thousands. Born in Cincinnati, Griffith grew up poor and left school after the eighth grade to help support her family. She took a job teaching in a sod schoolhouse in Nebraska, where she encountered families in which even the parents were unable to read, write, or do simple arithmetic. Griffith came to believe that education could lift struggling families out of poverty. She moved to Denver with her family in 1894 and began teaching there. From 1904 to 1908 she served as deputy state superintendent of schools. In 1916 Griffith convinced the Denver School Board to let her establish a free school with evening as well as daytime hours to serve both youth and adults. Now called the Emily Griffith Opportunity School, it serves immigrant and working-class populations with an emphasis on English language and vocational training. By the time Griffith retired as principal in 1933, the school had more than 8,600 students enrolled. After she retired, Griffith moved to Pinecliff, Colorado, to live with her sister. The two were found murdered at their mountain home on June 18, 1947. The crime was never solved. The Emily Griffith Opportunity School continues to operate, teaching basic job skill courses with the slogan "For All Who Wish to Learn."

JOHN WILLIAMS GUNNISON

PAINTING, HISTORY COLORADO

Soldier and explorer Captain John Williams
Gunnison (1812–53) gained posthumous fame as the
leader of a major railroad survey party. Gunnison
was born in Goshen, New Hampshire, in 1812 and
graduated from West Point in 1837. He began his
military career as an artillery officer in Florida,
where he spent a year in the campaign against the
Seminoles. During the 1840s Gunnison explored
and surveyed the area around the Great Lakes. In
the spring of 1849 he joined the Howard Stansbury
Expedition to the Valley of the Great Salt Lake. His
contact with Mormons in Utah led him to write a
book titled *The Mormons or Latter-Day Saints, in the
Valley of the Great Salt Lake: A History of Their Rise and
Progress, Peculiar Doctrines, Present Condition.* In June
1853 Gunnison led a survey party across the Rocky
Mountains along the Huerfano River, through
Cochetopa Pass, and along the river that now bears
his name. The party traversed the Tomichi Valley in
Colorado, where the town of Gunnison was named
in the explorer's honor. On the morning of October
26, 1853, Gunnison and his party were ambushed
by a band of Ute warriors near the banks of the
Sevier River in present-day Millard County, Utah.
Survivors of the attack reached another detachment
of the expedition and rode to aid Gunnison and
his party, only to recover eight mutilated bodies.
The site of the massacre was added to the National
Register of Historic Places in 1976.

JOHN F. HEALY

PAINTING, HISTORY COLORADO

John F. Healy (1873–1945) joined the Denver Fire Department in 1894 and served as Denver fire chief from 1912 to 1945. He was admired by the public, although some in the department considered him a tyrant. A dedicated firefighter, he was overcome by smoke so severely that he had to be hospitalized for weeks on six different occasions. Healy grew very attached to the horses that powered the department's fire trucks, and he mourned their replacement by motor-driven fire engines. Reluctantly, he oversaw the official retirement of the fire horses in 1924.

KATHARINE HEPBURN

PEN AND INK DRAWING, 1933, DENVER PUBLIC LIBRARY
WESTERN HISTORY AND GENEALOGY DEPARTMENT.
PUBLISHED IN THE WASHINGTON POST IN 1933.

Born on May 12, 1907, in Hartford, Connecticut, Katharine Hepburn (1907–2003) took up acting at Bryn Mawr College, appearing in many of the school's productions and finding small roles on Broadway soon after graduation. Notice for her role in *Art and Mrs. Bottle* (1931) led to stardom when she landed the key role of the Amazon princess Antiope in *A Warrior's Husband* (1932). *Little Women* (1933) was the most successful picture of its time, and in 1934 she won her first Oscar for *Morning Glory*. It was the beginning of a career filled with numerous awards. Hepburn eventually garnered twelve Oscar nominations and four wins, the latter still a record for an actress. This evocative pen and ink drawing by Herndon Davis celebrated her stage turn in Jed Harris's production of *The Lake* at the National Theatre in Washington, DC, in 1933.

JAMES BUTLER "WILD BILL" HICKOK

History Colorado

A skilled gunfighter, scout, and gambler, James Butler Hickok (1837–76)—known as "Wild Bill" Hickok—left his home in Illinois a fugitive from justice, ironically serving as a lawman in the frontier territories of Kansas and Nebraska. For a time he joined the "Free State Army" or "Jayhawkers"—anti-slavery guerrilla fighters who battled Missouri's pro-slavery "Border Ruffians." In 1859 he sustained serious injuries while battling a bear that blocked a freight team Hickok was leading from Independence, Missouri, to Santa Fe, New Mexico. During the Civil War he worked as a wagon master, a scout, and possibly a spy for the Union forces. Hickok was involved in several notable gun battles, including fights in which David McCanless was killed in 1861, Davis Tutt in 1865, and Phil Coe in 1871. In later years he tried his hand at acting and earned a living as a gambler. Hickok was shot to death from behind by a losing gambler while playing poker in a Deadwood, South Dakota, saloon.

HELEN HUNT JACKSON

PAINTING, HISTORY COLORADO

Poet and writer Helen Maria Hunt Jackson (1830–85) championed better treatment for Native Americans by the US government. Born Helen Fiske in Amherst, Massachusetts, she attended Ipswich Female Seminary, then the Abbott Institute in New York City. During her first marriage, to US Army captain Edward Bissell Hunt, the couple's two young children died from disease, and her husband met his untimely demise in an 1863 military accident. Helen began writing after losing her sons and her first husband. Sometime around 1873, Helen Hunt met William Sharpless Jackson, a wealthy banker and railroad executive, while visiting Colorado Springs. They married two years later.

Ralph Waldo Emerson admired her poetry and included five of her pieces in his anthology *Parnassus*. A 1879 lecture in Boston by the Ponca chief Standing Bear, in which he described the forcible removal of his people from their Nebraska reservation, captured Helen Jackson's imagination. She became an activist crusading against government mistreatment of American Indians. Her 1881 book, *A Century of Dishonor*, chronicled dirty tricks, massacres, and broken promises, documenting and exposing the corruption of US Indian agents, military officers, and settlers who encroached on and stole Indian lands. Jackson had a copy delivered to each member of Congress and made more than a few enemies with her outspoken activism. She followed this seminal work of nonfiction with *Ramona* (1884), a romantic novel about the struggles of a half-Indian orphan girl in Spanish California. *Ramona* was intended to generate sympathy for Native Americans among a broader readership than had the scholarly *Century of Dishonor*. Jackson was friends with Harriet Beecher Stowe, whose novel *Uncle Tom's Cabin* (1852) helped inspire *Ramona*. "If I could write a story that would do for the Indian one-hundredth part what *Uncle Tom's Cabin* did for the Negro, I would be thankful the rest of my life," she wrote.

Her writings, many of which focus on Colorado, did spur Washington to make attempts, not always successful, at humanizing US Indian policy. Helen published under both of her married names, Helen Hunt and Helen Jackson. She became Colorado's first great literary celebrity.

WILLIAM HENRY JACKSON
PAINTING, HISTORY COLORADO

Civil War veteran, photographer, painter, and explorer William Henry Jackson (1843–1942) became famous for his images of the American West. Born in Keeseville, New York, Jackson was a great-great-nephew of Samuel Wilson, the progenitor of America's national symbol, Uncle Sam. Jackson enlisted in the Union Army in 1862. After mustering out the following year, he went to work at a photographic gallery in Burlington, Vermont. Recovering from a broken heart in 1866, Jackson went west. He took a job as a bullwhacker for a freighting outfit based in Nebraska before opening his own photographic studio in Omaha in 1868. In 1869 the Union Pacific Railroad hired Jackson to photograph the scenery along its routes for promotional purposes. He was asked to join a geologic survey to explore the Yellowstone region in 1870, followed by an invitation to join the Hayden Geological Survey in 1871. The annual Hayden Surveys sought to chart and document the flora, fauna, and geology of the mostly unexplored West. As the official photographer for the survey, Jackson captured the first photographic documentation of the natural wonders of the West, which had heretofore seemed a matter of myth and legend to many easterners. His photographs, along with other documentation of the Hayden expedition, persuaded Congress in 1872 to establish Yellowstone National Park, the nation's first national park.

Jackson participated in each subsequent annual Hayden Survey until the final expedition in 1878. He established a studio in Denver, Colorado, where he compiled a huge inventory of national and international photography. From 1890 to 1892, Jackson again worked for several railroad lines, and in 1893 he was commissioned to photograph the World's Columbian Exposition in Chicago. From 1894 to 1896, Jackson produced more than 900 photographs as a member of and photographer for the World's Transportation Commission. Many original glass plate negatives of the most celebrated western photographer are in the Hart Library at the History Colorado Center in Denver.

ARTHUR LAKES

WATERCOLOR, 1961, DENVER PUBLIC LIBRARY AND GENEALOGY DEPARTMENT

A British-born geologist, educator, editor, artist, and Episcopal minister, the Reverend Arthur Lakes (1844–1917) attended Oxford before immigrating to Canada in 1865. He began teaching at the Colorado School of Mines in Golden in 1870. He is best remembered for his discovery of Jurassic age dinosaurs near Morrison, Colorado, in 1877. His find included the first known specimens of *Stegosaurus*, *Apatosaurus*, and *Diplodocus*. An amateur artist, Lakes sketched the dinosaurs he discovered and philosophized about art versus photography: "We have heard it argued that once photography in colors is discovered and in general use, the artist's occupation will be gone. No fear of that, the photographic machine has no heart, no soul, no poetry, no feeling, no love, and will never supplant the art of the human artist whose work of 'art' must be a work of 'heart,' be it in landscape, portraiture, or historical painting, for human nature to love or care for it" (Arthur Lakes, *Mines and Minerals*, 1902).

Lakes taught at the Colorado School of Mines, where the library is named for him. Davis painted this watercolor portrait for the booklet *History of Red Rocks Park and Theater*, by his friend and patron Nolie Mumey.

HERNDON R. DAVIS
UNITED STATES ARMY

DISTINGUISHED
FLYING
CROSS

CHARLES A. LINDBERGH

PEN AND INK DRAWING, 1927, DENVER PUBLIC LIBRARY WESTERN HISTORY AND GENEALOGY DEPARTMENT

The aviator, author, explorer, and activist Charles Augustus Lindbergh (1902–74) flew into the history books when, as a US Army Air Corps Reserve officer, he made the first solo transatlantic flight in 1927. Though his pro-German leanings in the late 1930s hurt his reputation, he remained a national hero, representing America's ascendancy in the world. The trial of his son's kidnapper-murderer gained him widespread sympathy. Herndon Davis's US Army recruitment poster won praise from military officers and art critics alike. It is a vibrant early example of the distinctive, nearly photo-realistic cross-stroke technique Davis was known for as a young illustrator.

BENJAMIN BARR LINDSEY

PAINTING, History Colorado

Benjamin Barr Lindsey (1869–1943) was a Progressive era judge and social reformer in Denver, Colorado. Born in Jackson, Tennessee, as a child Lindsey moved with his family to Denver, where he was educated in the public schools. While working in a real estate office, Lindsey studied law at night and entered legal practice in 1894. He was appointed to a vacancy in the county court in 1900 and served as judge until 1927. Lindsey created the world's second (after Chicago) juvenile court. He intended to rehabilitate, rather than merely punish, young lawbreakers. Lindsey also contributed to voter registration and electoral reform, the expansion of public parks, and the abolition of child labor. He promoted his progressive beliefs through speaking engagements and the publication of *The Beast* (1910), an indictment of Colorado's political system, coauthored with Harvey O'Higgins. This muckraking classic became a best-selling exposé of the corruption of Colorado's power elite and government.

Judge Lindsey ran unsuccessfully for governor of Colorado in 1906 and became a member of the Progressive National Committee in 1912. In 1927 Lindsey co-wrote a controversial book, *Companionate Marriage*, promoting trial marriage for young people, which drew heavy criticism. After Lindsey managed to offend the power elite, the churches, and conservatives, he was disbarred on trumped-up charges. He moved to Los Angeles, where he served on the County of Los Angeles Superior Court and continued to advocate for reform in the juvenile justice system, even making Hollywood movies promoting his liberal reform agenda.

HAROLD LLOYD

PAINTING, HISTORY COLORADO

Harold Lloyd (1893–1971), an influential comedian of the silent film era, was born in Burchard, Nebraska. He studied at Denver's East High School and in San Diego before beginning a film acting career. At the age of twelve, he played Little Abe in a local stage production of *Tess of the D'Urbervilles*. His first starring turn on the screen was in 1915's *Just Nuts*, in which he portrayed Willie Work, a knockoff of Charlie Chaplin's Little Tramp. In subsequent films Lloyd settled on a more original persona known as the "glasses" character, a resourceful go-getter in tune with 1920s' America. Lloyd made more than 200 comedy films between 1917 and 1947, both silent films and "talkies," but his greatest successes came before the advent of sound in cinema. He is considered one of the three comedic geniuses of silent film, along with Buster Keaton and Charlie Chaplin. The image of Lloyd dangling from a giant clock on the side of a building in his 1923 film *Safety Last!* became one of the indelible images of the silent film era. A founding member of the Academy of Motion Picture Arts and Sciences, he ultimately established his own production company.

BAT MASTERSON

PAINTING, HISTORY COLORADO

William Barclay "Bat" Masterson (1853–1921), a frontier lawman, gunfighter, US marshal, and writer, developed a mythic Old West persona. Born to an Irish immigrant family in what is now Henryville, Quebec, Masterson grew up the second of eight children. His family moved in search of farming prospects, finally settling near Wichita, Kansas. In his late teens, Bat slipped away from hunting buffalo with his brothers to join the Battle of Adobe Walls (June 27, 1874) in Texas, where he killed Comanche Indians. As a US Army scout, he joined a campaign against the Kiowa and Comanche Indians. In 1876 a love triangle gone wrong led to a shootout in which Bat killed both a soldier and the young woman for whom they had competed. Masterson took a bullet to the pelvis but recovered.

In 1877 he served as a sheriff's deputy alongside Wyatt Earp, and within a few months he was elected sheriff of Ford County, Kansas. While holding that office, he fought on the Santa Fe side against the Rio Grande Railroad in the Royal Gorge War (late 1870s). In 1878 he shot down cowboy Jack Wagner to avenge the killing of his brother Ed Masterson, marshal of Dodge City. Bat Masterson became a roving gambler, drifting through several legendary Old West locales. He worked a stint for Wyatt Earp in 1881 dealing faro at the Oriental Saloon in Tombstone, Arizona Territory. Masterson returned to law enforcement, serving a year as marshal of Trinidad, Colorado, followed by a term as sheriff of South Pueblo, Colorado.

Masterson became nationally famous as a Wild West gunfighter as the result of a practical joke played on a gullible newspaper reporter in August 1881. Seeking thrilling tales of the frontier in Gunnison, Colorado, the reporter asked Dr. W. S. Cockrell about notorious killers. Dr. Cockrell pointed to Bat, who happened to be nearby, and told the reporter he had killed twenty-six men. Cockrell told the reporter lurid, outlandish tales of Bat's exploits, which the reporter used in a story for the *New York Sun*. The story was widely reprinted and became the basis for even more wildly exaggerated legends about Masterson.

By 1888, Masterson was living in Denver, where he dealt cards before buying and managing the Palace Variety Theater. While in Denver he formed a friendship with the notorious confidence man Soapy Smith, with whom he collaborated on the infamous Denver registration and election fraud scandal of 1889. In Denver he also met the Native American nightclub singer Emma Moulton, who became Masterson's wife and companion for the rest of his life. Masterson spent his later years in New York City, writing a sports column, serving as a deputy US marshal, and trading off of his fame as a legend of the Old West.

FRED MAZZULLA

DRAWING, HISTORY COLORADO

Fred Mazzulla (1903–81) was an attorney, an independent historian, and a passionate collector of photos and documents from the Old West. Born in Trinidad, Mazzulla grew up in Salida. He and his wife, Jo, published several history booklets. They emphasized the sensational and the bawdy. In a 1972 interview, Mazzulla told *Denver Post* reporter Olga Curtis, "I'm no stickler for historical accuracy. Sometimes it takes showmanship to make history interesting." Mazzulla, a friend and patron of Herndon Davis, hired Davis to paint murals in his basement at 1930 East 8th Avenue, portraying notable figures from Colorado and western history, including Wild Bill Cody, Robert Speer, Soapy Smith, Horace Tabor and Elizabeth "Baby Doe" Tabor, Gene Fowler, Helen Bonfils, David Moffat, John Evans, William Byers, William M. Gilpin, and Joseph P. Machebeuf, among others. Much of the Mazzulla photo collection is now at History Colorado.

WILSON McCARTHY

DRAWING, HISTORY COLORADO

Wilson McCarthy (1884–1956), an attorney, jurist, and railroad executive, took receivership control of the bankrupt Denver and Rio Grande Western Railroad in 1934. Born to a Mormon family in Utah, McCarthy grew up a working cowboy in Alberta, Canada. Boots and western wear were standard attire for the rest of his life. After serving a church mission to his family's ancestral land, Ireland, McCarthy entered law school at Columbia University in 1910. After returning to Utah, McCarthy served as a judge and then went into private practice. In 1926 he was elected to the Utah State Senate. Following the Wall Street crash of 1929, McCarthy was appointed to the Resolution Finance Corporation (RFC). When the Denver and Rio Grande Western Railroad defaulted on a $10 million loan in 1934, RFC chairman Jess H. Jones asked McCarthy to take control of the railroad. For the next two decades, McCarthy oversaw the rehabilitation of the Rio Grande. By 1940 he had spent over $20 million upgrading the Rio Grande, building 1,130 bridges and laying over 2 million ties. Though passenger traffic declined as postwar America embraced the automobile, McCarthy increased freight traffic by developing agriculture and industry along the Rio Grande's routes to boost demand for shipping.

IDA KRUSE McFARLANE

PAINTING, HISTORY COLORADO

Ida Kruse McFarlane (1873–1940) was a Colorado educator and historic preservationist. Born in Central City, she taught English for thirty-three years at the University of Denver. A popular professor, she published some of her compiled lectures as *Modern Culture, the Arts of the Theatre* in 1919. McFarlane is best known for her efforts to rescue the Central City Opera from planned demolition in 1931. She enlisted the help of Anne Evans, daughter of the second territorial governor, John Evans. Evans was civically active and supported the performing arts, including the University of Denver's Civic Theater. With other volunteers, McFarlane and Evans founded the Central City Opera House Association (CCOHA) to save the historic structure, built by miners in 1877 when Central City claimed to be the "richest square mile on earth." After determining that the opera house was structurally sound, they approached the University of Denver with a plan to give the school title to the building. The plan took advantage of the university's tax-exempt status and its connection to the Civic Theater. The university agreed to McFarlane's gift, with the stipulation that it would have no responsibility for the upkeep or programming of the theater, tasks embraced by the CCOHA. McFarlane and the CCOHA first hosted a summer festival season that opened in 1932 with *Camille*, starring Lillian Gish. The festival became a great success and an annual affair, reviving not only the opera house but the town of Central City. McFarlane is commemorated on the University of Denver campus by a hall named for her. The CCOHA also owned and restored the adjacent Teller House Hotel, where Herndon Davis painted his famous *Face on the Barroom Floor*.

EDGAR CARLISLE McMECHAN

WATERCOLOR, HISTORY COLORADO

Edgar Carlisle McMechan (1884–1953), a journalist
who edited and wrote for Denver's *Municipal Facts*
magazine, became the principal public relations
man for Mayor Robert W. Speer. He later worked
as curator for the Denver Art Museum at Chappell
House and in 1934 became curator for the Colorado
History Museum (now History Colorado), where
he took a special interest in Elizabeth "Baby Doe"
Tabor material, Hispanic Colorado history, and
folk art during the Great Depression. McMechan
supervised the Works Progress Administration
(WPA) project to construct more than thirty history
dioramas at the museum, including the famous
1860 Denver diorama now on display at the new
History Colorado Center. He oversaw construction,
reconstruction, or renovation of History Colorado's
Pike's Stockade, Leadville's Healy House, Fort
Garland, and the Ute Indian Museum in Montrose.
McMechan published *The Moffat Tunnel of Colorado:
An Epic of Empire* in 1927 and flattering biographies
of Governor John Evans, Walter Scott Cheesman,
and Denver mayor Robert W. Speer. This Herndon
Davis watercolor portrait commemorated the "dour
little Scotsman" on his retirement from the Colorado
History Museum.

DAME NELLIE MELBA

WATERCOLOR, 1961, DENVER PUBLIC LIBRARY WESTERN HISTORY AND GENEALOGY DEPARTMENT

Dame Nellie Melba (1861–1931) was an Australian operatic soprano. Born Helen "Nellie" Porter Mitchell, she was renowned worldwide and became one of the most famous singers of her time. After studying singing in Melbourne, Melba moved to Europe where she continued her studies and found success in Paris and Brussels. She moved to London in 1888 and quickly established herself as the leading soprano at Covent Garden, before debuting in 1893 at the Metropolitan Opera in New York City. Melba was best known for her performances of French and Italian opera and seldom sang German operas. During World War I, she raised large sums of money for war relief charities. In 1910 she performed at what would become Red Rocks Amphitheatre in Morrison, Colorado. Impressed by the acoustics, she supposedly said, "This is the greatest open-air theatre I have ever seen." This 1961 illustration was created for *History of Red Rocks Park and Theater* by Nolie Mumey.

DAVID MOFFAT

PAINTING, HISTORY COLORADO

David Halliday Moffat (1839–1911), one of Colorado's most important financiers and industrialists in the late ninteenth and early twentieth centuries, was largely responsible for the early development of Middle Park and northwestern Colorado along his Moffat Railroad. Born in Washingtonville, New York, at age twelve he went to New York City and began his career in banking as a messenger boy for the New York Exchange Bank. He rose to the post of teller and cashier while working for banks in Des Moines, Iowa, before moving to the fledgling town of Denver, Colorado, in 1860 to open a bookstore at 15th and Larimer Streets. Soon he returned to banking and joined the First National Bank of Denver. He became cashier in 1867 and president in 1880, prevailing as the bank's controlling mind and personality until his death in 1911 in New York City.

Over the years, he held ownership positions in over 100 Colorado mines and nine railroads. The Denver Pacific Railway and Telegraph Company, founded in 1867 by Moffat, *Rocky Mountain News* editor William Byers, Governor John Evans, and others, linked Denver to the transcontinental line in Cheyenne. Moffat and Evans were also prime movers in the Denver, South Park and Pacific Railroad, started in 1872 to connect Denver with South Park and the mining districts. That narrow-gauge railroad opened up the first rail routes to a large section of the central Colorado mining districts.. The Denver and New Orleans Railroad, later known as the Denver, Texas and Gulf Railroad, was launched by Evans, Moffat, and other associates in 1881 to give Denver an outlet to shipping on the Gulf of Mexico. Moffat and Evans also partnered in the Denver Tramway Company in 1886, giving the city its major streetcar system. Moffat's great final effort focused on constructing a railroad due west from Denver to the Pacific Coast. His Denver, Salt Lake and Pacific, also known as the Moffat Road, strove to do just that. To circumvent difficult mountain passes, Moffat envisioned a tunnel through the Continental Divide west of Denver. His vision came to pass, but Moffat did not live to see it. Construction of the 6.2-mile-long Moffat Tunnel began in 1923, and it finally opened on February 28, 1928.

CHIEF OURAY

PAINTING, HISTORY COLORADO

Ouray (1833–80), chief of the Uncompahgre Utes of western Colorado, emerged as a spokesman for the entire Ute tribe. In the Ute language, according to oral history, Ouray means "the arrow." The future chief was supposedly given the name for the arrows of light made by a meteor shower the night of his birth. His father, Guera Murah, a Jicarilla Apache, married his mother (name unknown), an Uncompahgre Ute. Ouray mastered Spanish, English, and both the Ute and Apache languages, which helped make him a successful diplomat and peacemaker in the cultural crossroads of late-nineteenth-century Colorado. Secretary of the Interior Carl Schurtz, who oversaw US Indian affairs, called Ouray the smartest Indian he ever met.

Ouray and his first wife, Black Mare, had a son named Queashegut, but Black Mare died soon after his birth. Ouray went on to marry sixteen-year-old Chipeta, "White Singing Bird" in the Ute language. Sioux warriors who raided Ouray's buffalo-hunting camp near present-day Fort Lupton abducted Queashegut when he was five years old. Ouray never saw his son again and remained in grief over the loss for the rest of his life.

Ouray came to present-day Colorado to join his father's Tabeguache (Uncompahgre) Ute band. When his father died in 1860, Ouray became chief of the band at age twenty-seven. As chief, Ouray sought reconciliation between peoples, believing war with the whites would destroy the Ute tribe. Some Utes considered him a coward for seeking good relations with the expanding United States. In 1880 Ouray went to Washington, DC, to negotiate with government commissioners about a reservation for the Utes. Despite the huge public outcry after the Meeker Massacre to remove all Utes from Colorado, Ouray skillfully helped negotiate the establishment of the Southern Ute and Ute Mountain Ute Reservations in the state's southwest corner. He died on August 24, 1880, near the Los Pinos Indian Agency in Colorado.

WILLIAM PALMER

PAINTING, HISTORY COLORADO

William Jackson Palmer (1836–1909), an American civil engineer, soldier, industrialist, and philanthropist born in Leipsic, Delaware, became fascinated by steam engines as a child. At age seventeen he went to work building railroads in Pennsylvania, then he traveled to Europe to study railroad engineering and the use of coal rather than wood for steam locomotives. In 1856 he joined the Pennsylvania Railroad (PRR), where he gained the confidence of company president John Edgar Thomson. Based on his observations in Great Britain, Palmer convinced Thompson to switch the PRR to coal-fired rather than wood-burning engines, making it the first American railroad company to do so.

Palmer was a passionate abolitionist and, when the Civil War broke out, he overcame the pacifism of his Quaker upbringing to accept a commission as colonel in the Union Army. Confederate forces captured Palmer while he was spying after the Battle of Antietam (September 17, 1862) but returned him to his regiment in a February 1863 prisoner exchange. Palmer won accolades for his aggressive style as a battlefield commander, and in 1865 President Abraham Lincoln appointed him a brevet brigadier general. After the war, Palmer generously donated money to support education for freed former slaves.

Palmer resumed his railroad career in the West, building the Kansas Pacific Railroad from Kansas City to Denver. In 1867 he met Dr. William Bell, who became his friend and partner in many business ventures. Together they co-founded the Denver and Rio Grande Railroad, which eventually operated the largest network of narrow-gauge railroads in the United States. Palmer helped develop rail-related industries in Colorado, including coal mining and what became the Colorado Fuel and Iron Company, which constructed a huge steel mill in Pueblo. He founded Colorado Springs in 1871, gracing his adopted home with philanthropy that supported education, parks, and other public amenities.

SPENCER PENROSE

PAINTING, HISTORY COLORADO

Spencer Penrose (1865–1939) was an entrepreneur, venture capitalist, and philanthropist who transformed Colorado Springs into a tourist haven. Born into a prominent Philadelphia family, Penrose graduated last in his class at Harvard and had a reputation as a drinker and a lady's man. He came to Colorado to run a real estate office in Cripple Creek with his longtime partner, Charles L. Tutt. They struck it rich with their C.O.D. Mine, the first major Cripple Creek jackpot. Realizing that ore processing outshone mining as a sure financial bet, Penrose also developed a large smelting operation in Colorado City to process gold ore from Cripple Creek, the richest gold mining district in the world for a few years around 1900. Penrose augmented his fortune by collaborating with his geologist brother's gold and silver Commonwealth Mine in Pearce, Arizona. The Penrose brothers also bought into a Bingham Canyon, Utah, property that held enormous reserves of low-grade copper ore. His investment in the Bingham Copper Mine near Salt Lake City paid handsomely for decades from what became the biggest pit mine in North America.

Penrose financed many of the most prominent landmarks in Colorado Springs, including the Broadmoor Hotel, the Cheyenne Mountain Zoo, the Will Rogers Shrine of the Sun, the Pikes Peak Highway, and the Glockner-Penrose Hospital. His wife, Julie, was an ardent supporter of the performing and visual arts and a major supporter of the Central City Opera and the Colorado Springs Fine Arts Center. The Broadmoor Hotel (1918) remains the state's premier resort hotel, and most of the other attractions Penrose established to bring tourists to Colorado Springs thrive to this day. In 1937 the couple set up El Pomar Foundation, the largest in the state for decades, to fund needy Colorado causes.

ZEBULON MONTGOMERY PIKE
PAINTING, History Colorado

Zebulon Montgomery Pike (1779–1813) was an American military officer and explorer for whom Colorado's Pikes Peak is named. Born in New Jersey, Pike followed in the footsteps of his father, also named Zebulon, who fought in the Revolutionary War. In 1799 the younger Pike joined his father's regiment and earned a commission as ensign in 1804. As a US Army captain in 1806–7, he led an expedition to map and explore the southern portion of the Louisiana Territory. The team attempted, without success, to climb the majestic mountain that would later be called Pikes Peak. After crossing into Spanish territory, Pike's expedition ended abruptly with its arrest by Spanish authorities. After being detained and questioned as a spy in Mexico, Pike was released in 1807 at the Louisiana border. Pike published an account of his journey in 1810, which became a best-seller in both the United States and Europe. His star rose within the US Army as well. As a lieutenant colonel, Pike fought at the Battle of Tippecanoe (November 7, 1811) with the 4th Infantry Regiment. He was promoted to the rank of brigadier general during the War of 1812 and died in action during the American victory at the Battle of York (present-day Toronto) in 1813.

WILLIAM McLEOD RAINE

PAINTING, HISTORY COLORADO

London-born William McLeod Raine (1871–1954)
moved to Arkansas with his family as a ten-year-
old child and became a popular novelist of the
American Old West. After being educated at Oberlin
College, he moved to Denver to work as a reporter
and editor for several local newspapers while he
transitioned into freelance fiction writing. His early
novels were historical romances set in the English
countryside, but Raine found his voice with the
1908 publication of *Wyoming*. In a career that lasted
until his death in Denver in 1954, Raine averaged
almost two western novels per year. During World
War I, a half million copies of his books were distributed to British soldiers in the trenches. Twenty
of his books have been made into movies. Though
his output was prodigious, Raine considered himself a slow, careful, and accurate wordsmith.

RED TOMAHAWK

DRAWING, HISTORY COLORADO

Native American warrior turned Bureau of Indian Affairs tribal police officer Chief Red Tomahawk (1853?–1931) is best known for killing the Sioux chief Sitting Bull in 1890. Tacanipiluta (Red Tomahawk) was born sometime around 1853 in the Montana Territory. His mother was Lakota and his father belonged to the Ihanktowana Dakota (also known as Yanktonai) tribe. As a young man, Red Tomahawk hunted bison with his people and participated in fights against soldiers, settlers, and miners encroaching on their land.

By the late 1880s, native resistance to white encroachment had been virtually ended, and Red Tomahawk had become a sergeant of Indian police at Fort Yates, North Dakota. When the apocalyptic Ghost Dance movement swept western tribes in 1890, government officials became anxious about renewed uprisings and targeted the Lakota Sioux chief Sitting Bull, despite the fact that he had surrendered to the United States more than nine years earlier. On December 15, 1890, Bureau of Indian Affairs agent James McLaughlin ordered Red Tomahawk and Lieutenant Bull Head to arrest Sitting Bull at the Standing Rock Agency in North Dakota, where the chief was camped with his people. A force of forty-three police agents rousted the chief from his bed at 6:00 a.m., but an angry crowd gathered as the agents attempted to forcibly remove him from the camp. When a Lakota shouldered his rifle and shot Bull Head, Red Tomahawk fired his gun into Sitting Bull's head, killing him. A furious battle ensued, with Red Tomahawk taking charge of the police force until cavalry support arrived. Red Tomahawk became famous for slaying Sitting Bull, who had shown almost super-human prowess on the battlefield in days gone by. He continued to serve as a police officer until 1895, gaining the rank of captain.

H.R. DAVIS
1929

Red Stonechaw

FRANKLIN D. ROOSEVELT AND HERBERT HOOVER

PEN AND INK DRAWING, 1932, DENVER PUBLIC LIBRARY
WESTERN HISTORY AND GENEALOGY DEPARTMENT.
PUBLISHED NOVEMBER 22, 1932, IN THE *WASHINGTON
DAILY NEWS*.

This illustration, juxtaposing portraits of the thirty-first and thirty-second presidents of the United States, ran with news of an unprecedented transition meeting between president-elect Franklin D. Roosevelt and his recent opponent, the lame duck president Herbert Hoover. In the face of a deepening banking crisis at the nadir of the Great Depression, three such meetings took place in the long interim between Roosevelt's fall 1932 election victory and spring 1933 inauguration. Yet Roosevelt refrained from co-signing any of Hoover's prescribed actions to forestall the crisis, waiting instead until the first day of his administration to begin the process of restoring confidence with his enforced "bank holiday." The artist Davis easily captures the contrasting spirits of the gregarious Roosevelt and the stiff, defeated Hoover.

JOHN L. ROUTT

PAINTING, HISTORY COLORADO

John Long Routt (1826–1907), the last territorial governor and first state governor of Colorado, also served a term as mayor of Denver. Born in Eddyville, Kentucky, Routt apprenticed as a carpenter, then entered politics when he was elected sheriff of McLean County in 1860. He served with distinction in the Civil War as captain of the 94th Illinois Volunteer Regiment. His valor at the Battles of Prairie Grove (December 7, 1862) and Vicksburg (May 18–July 4, 1863) earned him promotion to the rank of colonel. On March 29, 1875, President Ulysses S. Grant appointed Routt to the territorial governorship of Colorado. When Colorado became the thirty-eighth state in the Union the following year, Routt was elected the state's first governor, a post he held from 1876 to 1879. At the end of his term he did not seek reelection, returning instead to his mining and ranching interests. Routt did not stay away from politics for long, though; he served as mayor of Denver from 1883 to 1885 and was reelected to the governor's office in 1891. After leaving office in 1893, Routt put his energies into a successful campaign to expand the voting franchise to women in Colorado. Governor John L. Routt died in Denver on August 13, 1907.

DAMON RUNYON

PAINTING, HISTORY COLORADO

Alfred Damon Runyon (1880–1946), an American newspaperman and author, was born in Manhattan, Kansas, and grew up in Pueblo, Colorado, where he worked as a reporter for the *Pueblo Chieftain*. He later moved to Denver, where he wrote for the *Rocky Mountain News* and then the *Denver Post*. Runyon relocated to New York City in 1910, where he worked for various newspapers before becoming a columnist for the Hearst papers. He was best known for his short stories celebrating the world of Broadway in New York City during the Prohibition era. To New Yorkers of his generation, the adjective "Runyonesque" evoked a distinctly hedonistic or bohemian social type, including gamblers, hustlers, actors, and gangsters, portrayed in a distinctive vernacular style. Runyon's fictional world is best known to the general public through the musical *Guys and Dolls*, based on several of his stories, including "The Idyll of Miss Sarah Brown," "Blood Pressure," and "Pick the Winner." The film *Little Miss Marker* is based on his short story with the same name.

JEFFERSON RANDOLPH "SOAPY" SMITH

PAINTING, HISTORY COLORADO

Jefferson Randolph "Soapy" Smith II (1860–98) became famous as a con artist, saloon and gambling-house proprietor, gangster, and crime boss who operated primarily in Colorado and Alaska. His most famous scam, selling soap bars supposedly wrapped with big dollar bills inside, gave him the nickname "Soapy." Winners who loudly proclaimed that their purchased soap bars had big bucks inside were Smith's confederates. When arrested for this scam, Colorado's most notorious con artist was allegedly booked under the name "Soapy" Smith. He is best known for his role in the organized criminal operations of Denver, Leadville, and Creede, Colorado, and Skagway, Alaska. In Denver, Smith and his gang ran saloons, gambling halls, cigar stores, auction houses, and a fake mining company that fleeced their customers. Smith also became involved in politics, "fixing" city, county, and state elections. In 1894, Populist governor Davis Waite confronted Smith and his clique during the bloodless "City Hall War." Soapy subsequently moved on to ply his nefarious trades in Skagway, Alaska, where he was slain in a shootout on July 8, 1898. His saloon and grave are major Skagway tourist attractions.

ROBERT SPEER

PAINTING, HISTORY COLORADO

Robert Walter Speer (1855–1918) served ten years as mayor of Denver, Colorado. Born in Mount Union, Pennsylvania, Speer moved to Denver as a young adult in 1880, searching for a healthy climate to help his tuberculosis. After stints as a store clerk and a real estate agent, he embarked on a career in politics, and was elected city clerk the year he arrived in town. In 1885 President Grover Cleveland named Speer postmaster for Denver, a position he held for six years. In 1891 Speer became a board member of the Denver police and fire departments, which gave him oversight of liquor licenses—and a following among Denver's underworld. His demimonde connections paid off with his election as mayor of Denver in 1904, thanks to thousands of fraudulent ballots cast with the help of the corporate executives, saloon keepers, gambling-hall operators, and prostitutes he protected.

Though Speer was allegedly corrupt, it cannot be denied that he left Denver a lasting legacy of civic improvements. An adherent of the City Beautiful Movement, he helped change Denver from a dusty western boomtown into an aesthetically attractive modern city, a "Paris on the Platte," as he put it. He cleared several blocks west of the state capitol to create Civic Center Park, featuring stately neoclassic design. He distributed over 110,000 free trees to Denver residents to plant in their yards. Speer cleared the streets of unsightly wires and billboards, giving the downtown distinctive streetlights and a welcome arch for Union Station. He built fine public buildings, such as the Museum of Natural History in City Park and the Municipal Auditorium at 14th and Curtis Streets, which hosted everything from political conventions to free Sunday concerts. Speer died in 1918 during his third term as Denver's mayor, but his lasting influence can still be seen throughout the city, including the arterial boulevard along Cherry Creek that bears his name. His City Beautiful plan created Civic Center, doubled Denver's park acreage, and created parkways and a 14,000-acre Denver Mountain Parks network outside the city in the mountains west of town.

BENJAMIN FRANKLIN STAPLETON

PAINTING, HISTORY COLORADO

Benjamin Franklin Stapleton (1869–1950) sat in the Denver mayor's chair for a total of five terms, from 1923 to 1931 and from 1935 to 1947. He also held the post of Colorado state auditor from 1933 to 1935. Born in Paintsville, Kentucky, Stapleton earned a law degree in Ohio. In the early 1890s he came to Denver and was admitted to the Colorado Bar in 1899. After volunteering with the First Colorado Regiment during the Spanish-American War, he returned to his Denver law practice, then pivoted to politics. He became police magistrate from 1904 to 1915, when President Woodrow Wilson appointed him postmaster.

Deep infiltration of Colorado political and civic institutions by the Ku Klux Klan led Stapleton to court the "Invisible Empire" during his first campaign for mayor in 1923. Though he publicly denied it, Stapleton became a Klan member and befriended Colorado Klan grand dragon John Galen Locke. Stapleton enjoyed the strong support of the Klan, and he appointed fellow Klansmen to multiple positions in Denver's government after his election victory. An anti-Stapleton backlash developed in 1924, forcing a recall election in which Stapleton openly campaigned on his Klan loyalties and prevailed over a weak opponent. Shortly afterward, Stapleton denounced the Klan and dropped his membership.

After a stint as state auditor, Stapleton ran for mayor again in 1935 and won. Many public improvements were made during his tenure, most of which came during the Great Depression years when the federal New Deal placed funds and labor at the mayor's disposal. Projects accomplished during Stapleton's administration include the creation of the Denver Municipal Airport, as well as the expansion of the Denver Mountain Parks system, including construction of the amphitheatre at Red Rocks Park. Denver Municipal Airport was renamed for Stapleton in 1944.

BELLE STARR

PENCIL WITH WATERCOLOR ACCENTS ON PAPER, 1961,
DENVER PUBLIC LIBRARY WESTERN HISTORY AND
GENEALOGY DEPARTMENT

Belle Starr (1848–89), born Myra Maybelle Shirley
on her father's farm near Carthage, Missouri, grew
up to be a notorious Wild West outlaw. Known as
a crack shot, Belle rode sidesaddle in a black vel-
vet riding habit and a plumed hat. She carried two
pistols, with cartridge belts slung across her hips.
In the 1860s she associated with Jesse James, the
Younger Brothers, and pro-Confederate criminal
gangs. In 1866 she married gangster Jim Reed but
was widowed when he died in a shootout in 1871.
In 1880 she married Sam Starr, a Cherokee, and
settled with his family in the Indian Territory. The
two were tried for horse theft in 1883, and Belle
served time behind bars. Belle Starr was murdered
by an unknown assailant on February 3, 1889, in an
ambush near Eufaula, Oklahoma. Dime-store novelist Richard K. Fox made Starr nationally famous
when he published *Bella Starr, the Bandit Queen, or
the Female Jesse James* the year she died. The reason
for altering Starr's first name from Belle to "Bella" is
unclear; perhaps it was intended to make the subject
seem more exotic or to invoke the Spanish meaning
of bella: beautiful.

WINFIELD SCOTT STRATTON

PAINTING, HISTORY COLORADO

Winfield Scott Stratton (1848–1902), a carpenter, prospector, mine owner, and philanthropist, was born in Jeffersonville, Indiana. Stratton came to Colorado Springs in 1869 to work as a carpenter. After years of unsuccessful prospecting, Stratton finally discovered the Independence Lode near Victor, Colorado, on July 4, 1891, and became the Cripple Creek district's first millionaire. Stratton was generous with his windfall; he paid for food and shelter for the thousands left homeless by the Cripple Creek fire in 1896 and wrote generous checks to fellow "bonanza kings" down on their luck, "Crazy Bob" Womack and Horace A. Tabor. In time, Stratton turned reclusive and eccentric, reading, drinking, and shunning the company of others.

In 1900 the Venture Corporation of London bought Stratton's Independence Mine for $10 million. The Venture Corporation sold shares on the London Stock Exchange—shares that crashed later that year when the ore reserves were discovered to be less substantial than previously thought. Later lawsuits against the Stratton estate, claiming that the mine had been salted, were ruled in Stratton's favor by US courts. Stratton died on September 14, 1902, leaving the bulk of his estate for the establishment of the Myron Stratton Home in Colorado Springs for "the aged poor and dependent children," named for his father, Myron Stratton. Colorado places named for him include a hall at the School of Mines, a spring in Manitou Springs, a street, school, and post office in Colorado Springs, and a town in Kit Carson County.

ELIZABETH "BABY DOE" TABOR

PAINTING, HISTORY COLORADO

Elizabeth McCourt Doe Tabor (1854–1935) became famous as "Baby Doe" Tabor, the second wife of pioneer Colorado silver mining magnate, entrepreneur, and politician Horace A.W. Tabor. Born in Oshkosh, Wisconsin, Elizabeth McCourt came to Central City, Colorado, in 1877 with her first husband, Harvey Doe. The miners found Elizabeth so beautiful that they nicknamed her "Baby Doe." She soon gained a reputation as one of the most flamboyant and alluring women in the mining districts. Harvey Doe mined for gold without success, went into debt, and began drinking, gambling, and visiting brothels, leading his wife to sue for divorce. Elizabeth moved to Leadville, Colorado, where she met Horace Tabor, a wealthy "Silver King." They fell in love, despite the fact that Tabor was married. In 1883 he scandalously divorced Augusta Tabor, his wife of twenty-five years, to marry Baby Doe, who was half his age.

The Tabors had two daughters and enjoyed a lavish lifestyle made possible by Horace's rich silver mines. Tabor invested heavily in other mining companies and built grand architectural testaments to his wealth, such as the Tabor Grand Opera House in downtown Denver. Horace and Elizabeth's whirlwind decade of expensive clothes, parties, and travel came to an end in 1893. The repeal of the Sherman Silver Purchase Act caused Colorado's silver-based economy to crash, leaving the region filled with bankruptcies and dashed dreams. The over-leveraged Tabor was no exception. He died in reduced circumstances and Baby Doe returned to Leadville with her two daughters, Elizabeth "Lily" and Rose Mary "Silver Dollar." Loyal to her husband and attached to a delusional fantasy that their wealth could somehow be regained, she obtained permission from the new owners of the Matchless Mine, once a crown jewel in her husband's empire, to live in the mine's small supply cabin. She dwelt there as a virtual hermit for the reminder of her life, until found frozen to death after a snowstorm in March 1935 at age eighty-one.

HORACE AUSTIN WARNER TABOR

PAINTING, HISTORY COLORADO

A prospector, businessman, and politician, Horace Austin Warner Tabor (1830–99) became known as the Bonanza King of Leadville. Born in Vermont, Tabor made his way to Colorado by way of Kansas. In January 1856, Tabor was elected to Kansas's Free-State Topeka Legislature, but that body was soon unseated by President Franklin Pierce in favor of a pro-slavery legislature elected with underhanded tactics by "Border Ruffians" from Missouri. From 1860 to 1878, Tabor made a living in the Leadville area as a merchant and miner. By "grubstaking" miners, Tabor gained shares in successful mines and became very wealthy during the Leadville silver boom. His extravagant spending caused discord with his first wife, Augusta Tabor, and their divorce and his subsequent marriage to Elizabeth McCourt Doe, better known as "Baby Doe," scandalized Victorian-era Colorado. Tabor served one term as lieutenant governor of Colorado (1879–83) and one month as a US senator, filling out Henry Teller's term after his appointment as secretary of the interior. Tabor used his wealth to build Denver's now-demolished Tabor Grand Opera House and the still standing Leadville Opera House and to invest in mining and real estate before the 1893 silver crash and resulting economic depression in Colorado nearly wiped him out. He died in a small room in the Windsor Hotel in 1899.

HENRY HEYE TAMMEN

PAINTING, HISTORY COLORADO

Harry Heye Tammen (1856–1924), co-founder, co-owner, and co-publisher of the *Denver Post,* was born the son of a German immigrant pharmacist in Baltimore, Maryland. He was educated in Baltimore and worked in Philadelphia before moving to Denver in 1880. Tammen tended bar at the Windsor Hotel before establishing the firm H. H. Tammen & Co. in 1881. This curio shop focused on mineral specimens, Native American materials, postcards, and other souvenirs of the West. Tammen had a passion for mineralogy and around 1882 published a promotional journal called *Western Echoes*, "Devoted to Mineralogy, Natural History, Botany, &c. &c."

In 1895 Tammen partnered with Frederick G. Bonfils to buy the floundering *Denver Evening Post* for $12,500. As co-owners and co-editors, they turned the renamed *Denver Post* into the largest and most powerful of the six Denver dailies at the turn of the century. Under Tammen and Bonfils, the *Post* gained a reputation for red-ink headlines and yellow journalism; the *Post*'s downtown office was known as "the Bucket of Blood." "The public not only likes to be fooled—it insists upon it," was Tammen's reported mantra. The *Post* posed as the people's champion, "the Paper with a Heart and Soul," but was not above using its power to undercut its enemies and reap financial gain through unethical means. Tammen died in 1924, leaving the paper under the control of the Bonfils family. Tammen left millions of dollars to Children's Hospital to support care for the underprivileged.

HENRY MOORE TELLER

PAINTING, HISTORY COLORADO

Henry Moore Teller (1830–1914), a Colorado politician, served as a US senator from 1876 to 1882 and 1885–1909 and as US secretary of the interior from 1882 to 1885. Born in New York to a prominent old Dutch family, he trained as an attorney before moving to Central City in 1861. There, Teller opened a law practice and prospered representing various mining interests. He also became a major supporter of the Colorado Central Railroad, which served the Clear Creek mining towns.

In the US Senate, Teller championed silver mining, Colorado's leading industry. He argued for a bimetallic standard based on both gold and silver. After 1873 legislation shifted the United States to the gold standard, Senator Teller pushed the federal silver purchase acts that subsidized silver mining and required federal purchases. In 1892 he was instrumental in securing a declaration by the Republican National Convention in favor of bimetallism. At the next Republican National Convention, in 1896, Teller led a revolt against the party platform when it failed to support silver coinage. So-called Silver Republicans wanted Teller nominated for president, but they were outnumbered by supporters of William McKinley. After McKinley's nomination, Teller joined other leading Silver Republicans in a statement supporting the Democratic ticket. Teller became a Democrat, serving the remainder of his years in the Senate as a member of that party.

Teller was also known for his strong opposition to the Dawes Act (1887), a law intended to break up communal Native American lands and force assimilation into the Anglo-Saxon way of life. The Dawes Act called for allotment, which meant granting small plots of communal land to individual Indian owners and selling the "excess" to the government. Teller believed allotment was meant "to despoil the Indians of their lands and to make them vagabonds on the face of the earth." Teller said, "The real aim of this bill is to get at the Indian lands and open them up to settlement. The provisions for the apparent benefit of the Indians are but the pretext to get at his [sic] lands and occupy them." Yet as secretary of the interior in 1883, Teller approved a harsh "Code of Indian Offenses," which prohibited Native American traditional ceremonial activity, such as sacred dances, until its repeal by Indian commissioner John Collier in 1934. The Teller House in Central City and Teller County honor Teller's memory.

JOHN THOMPSON

John Edward Thompson (1882–1945) was born in Buffalo, New York. He studied art in New York and France. In 1917 he moved to Colorado to paint landscapes. He taught at the Denver Academy of Fine and Applied Arts and founded the Chappell School of Fine Art at 1300 Logan Street. He executed decorative paintings in the homes of Denver's wealthy and in public buildings. His paintings focused on nature, especially mountains, but he also did portraits and still lifes. One of Denver's most influential modernist artists, he ended his career teaching at the University of Denver.

TOM TOBIN

Thomas Tate Tobin (1823–1904) was a mountain man, trapper, guide, US Army scout, and occasional bounty hunter. Tobin explored southern Colorado with men such as Kit Carson, Richens L. "Uncle Dick" Wootton, Ceran St. Vrain, Charles Bent, and John C. Frémont. Tobin barely escaped death at the siege of Turley's Mill during the Taos Revolt in 1847. In 1864 he tracked down and killed the notorious Felipe Espinosa and his brother, José, who had been terrorizing Anglo settlers in southern Colorado. Tobin brought their heads back to Fort Garland in a sack to collect the "dead or alive" bounty.

JOHN BRISBEN WALKER

WATERCOLOR, 1940, DENVER PUBLIC LIBRARY WESTERN HISTORY AND GENEALOGY DEPARTMENT. PUBLISHED IN THE *ROCKY MOUNTAIN NEWS*, AUGUST 25, 1940.

John Brisben Walker (1847–1931), a businessman of many and varied pursuits, was at various times an inventor, a general, a politician, and a newspaper editor, as well as an investor and real estate developer. He developed Denver's first amusement park, River Front Park, where he staged the city's first rodeo, among other attractions. In the 1880s he donated the land that has become the campus of Regis University. After a successful stint in publishing in New York City, Walker returned west to Colorado and concentrated on developing the Red Rocks area. His dream of building a Summer White House for US presidents on Mount Falcon was never realized. Walker was one of the visionaries who created the Denver Mountain Parks system, which included his Red Rocks Park.

GEORGE WASHINGTON

This undated pen drawing of George Washington (1732–99), Revolutionary War hero and the first president of the United States, is intricate and carefully studied, creating depth and texture. It almost certainly belongs to the earlier years of Davis's career.

ELLA "CATTLE KATE" WATSON

PENCIL WITH WATERCOLOR ACCENTS ON PAPER, 1961,
HISTORY COLORADO

Ella Watson (1861–89), a Wyoming pioneer, became
the subject of dubious accusations of cattle rus-
tling. The popular characterization of Watson as
an "outlaw" was a stretch because she was not
violent and was never charged with any crime. At
age sixteen she escaped an abusive marriage in
Nebraska, then moved the following year to join her
family in Denver. With her second husband, James
"Jim" Averell, she homesteaded and ranched near
Rawlins, Wyoming, in the 1880s. The couple butted
heads with the powerful Wyoming Stock Growers
Association, which used its control of the cattle
branding system for unfair advantage and made
bogus homesteading claims to squeeze out smaller
competitors. Watson and Averell were targeted by
false accusations of smuggling and were lynched
by agents of this powerful cattle ranchers' syndicate
for opposing their interests. Watson's legendary life
and death helped incite the Johnson County War
(1889–93).

FRANCES "PINKY" WAYNE

PAINTING, HISTORY COLORADO

Frances Belford "Pinky" Wayne (1870–1951) was
a crusading journalist whose career in Colorado
newspapers spanned forty-five years. Born in
Boston, the daughter of Colorado's first US representative, James Belford, she split her time between
Central City, Colorado, and Washington, DC. She
joined the staff of the *Rocky Mountain News* in 1906
as a music and drama critic. After a brief marriage to educator Anthony Wayne and a stint at
the *Chicago Examiner,* Frances Wayne returned to
Denver in 1908 and went to work for the *Denver
Post.* Known as an opinionated and crusading
journalist, Wayne tackled topics usually covered
by men, including crime, politics, and coal miners' strikes. Wayne also wrote passionately about
issues important to women, including women's and
children's rights and birth control. Her articles in
support of reformers Emily Griffith and Judge Ben
Lindsey helped shape public opinion in favor of
their projects. In 1944 she successfully challenged
Colorado governor John Vivian to appoint a prominent woman scientist, Dr. Florence Sabin, to his
post–World War II planning committee. Wayne was
capable of embracing lighter themes as well: in 1918
she organized an outdoor Christmas lighting con-
test that ignited a city-wide craze. At age seventy-six
she was fired from the *Post* after a dispute with her
managing editor. She returned to her childhood
home, Central City, where she succumbed to cancer
in 1951.

EDWARD O. WOLCOTT

PAINTING, HISTORY COLORADO

Edward Oliver Wolcott (1848–1905) served as an attorney, politician, and US senator from Colorado. Born in Longmeadow, Massachusetts, to a prominent old family, he served in the Union Army during the Civil War and afterward graduated from Harvard Law School. In 1871 he moved to Black Hawk, Colorado, where he taught school and practiced law. He moved to Georgetown in 1871 and then to Denver in 1879. As an attorney, he worked for many major corporations, including the Denver and Rio Grande Railroad and big mining companies. He was elected district attorney and later to the Colorado State Senate. He held one of Colorado's US Senate seats from 1889 to 1901. Known as a bon vivant, he died on the French Riviera.

SANTOS

Traditional New Mexican *santos* are carved cottonwood or pine sculptures (*bultos*) or painted wood panels (*retalbos*) representing Christ, the Virgin Mary, saints, and other religious figures. The first Spanish settlers brought religious images with them to New Mexico in 1598 and imported more during the seventeenth century. Settlers and their churches possessed sculptures, paintings on canvas or copper, engravings, and gilded tabernacles. Many such Christian images were destroyed in the Pueblo Uprising of 1680.

In the 1700s the Spanish restored settler communities in what is now New Mexico. These villages developed their own unique style of holy images, grounded in the Spanish Catholic tradition, the evolving art styles of Europe, and local influences. Instead of imported marble, gold, and other rich materials, they used local wood for altars, *retalbos*, and *santos*. These saints or holy ones took their place along with imported pieces in homes and churches on the northern frontier of New Spain. At least a dozen saint-makers, or *santeros*, were active in New Mexico by the 1820s. The distinctive aesthetic created by the *santeros* eventually drew the interest of secular art collectors. An early-twentieth-century revival of interest in Hispanic art and culture led to a rebirth of *santeros* and widespread collecting and museum displays of these figures.

Dr. Nolie Mumey (1891–1984), a Denver surgeon and western historian, possessed one of the nation's largest collections of *santos*. In 1961 he hired his friend Herndon Davis to paint them in oils. Davis created a series of images unlike any other known in his career to commemorate Mumey's collection. Davis's respect for the unique aesthetics of the New Mexican artisan tradition—including alternately bold and moody uses of color from a distinctively southwestern palate—marks a striking new departure for his art, only a year before his untimely death. In 1984 Mumey donated seventy-eight of these paintings to the Western History and Genealogy Department of the Denver Public Library.

CARRETA MUERTE

Denver Public Library Western History and Genealogy Department

The "death cart" was a featured vehicle of Los Hermanos Penitentes, a New Mexican Catholic sect that developed in the absence of clergy and close supervision from the Roman church hierarchy. Brothers of the Penitentes order believed in self-flagellation and would sometimes pull wagons full of stones behind them with one hand while whipping themselves with the other. The figure in the cart symbolized the angel of death, and his bow and arrow represented an unexpected swift death.

CHRISTO ENTIERRO

This *santo* presents a stylized representation of a
buried Christ.

DEVOTION TO THE HOLY FAMILY OF JESUS, MARY, AND JOSEPH

Devotion to the Holy Family of Jesus, Mary, and Joseph
was promoted in New Mexico by a religious confra-
ternity called the Sons of the Holy Family (Coros de la
Sagrada Familía), which originated in Spain in 1864.

GOOD SHEPHERD

Denver Public Library Western History and Genealogy Department

In scripture, Christ is often portrayed as the "Good Shepherd" who carefully tends his flock of followers. The image of the shepherd has been prominent in Christian art through the centuries.

LUCIFER

DENVER PUBLIC LIBRARY WESTERN HISTORY AND
GENEALOGY DEPARTMENT

The devil is represented in Dr. Mumey's *santo* collection by this winged figure of the fallen angel who turned diabolical and rules hell.

SAN ACACIO

Denver Public Library Western History and Genealogy Department

San Acacio (died ca. 303), or Acacius in Latin, was a centurion in the Roman army who was crucified for converting to Christianity. San Acacio plays a major role in the community traditions of Mexican Catholics in Colorado's San Luis Valley, who trace their roots to New Mexico. According to legend, a New Mexican village attacked by the Utes was saved by the miraculous appearance of San Acacio and his Roman legion.

SAN ANTONIO

Antony Manzi the Pilgrim (ca. 1237–67), also known as St. Anthony of Padua, came from a wealthy family but gave his inheritance to the poor, thereby alienating his family. He lived as a pilgrim, wandering around Europe in the greatest austerity. When miracles occurred at his gravesite, the faithful of Padua sought to have him canonized. His feast day is June 13.

SAN FRANCISCO

Denver Public Library Western History and Genealogy Department

Saint Francis of Assisi (ca. 1181–1226) is one of the most beloved and revered of all the saints. As a youth, Francis pursued pleasure and high living. He was transformed by a pilgrimage to Rome in 1206, after which he devoted himself to a life of poverty and service to the sick and the poor. His compassion for animals has made him a favorite with animal lovers and his statue a popular garden ornament. He formed a monastic order in 1216 and made several, mostly unsuccessful attempts to evangelize Muslims in Tunis, Morocco, Egypt, and Palestine. He received the stigmata in 1224, one of many supernatural events reported in his lifetime. His feast day is October 4.

SAN ISIDRO

Denver Public Library Western History and
Genealogy Department

San Isidro, or Isidore the Farmer (ca. 1070–1130), is
the patron saint of farmers. Isidro was a Spanish
laborer known for his piety toward the poor and
toward animals. While resting from his plowing, an
angel miraculously appeared to plow for him. Ever
since, farmers have prayed to San Isidro for help.
His feast day is celebrated May 15.

SAN JOSE

Denver Public Library Western History and
Genealogy Department

In the gospels, Saint Joseph was the husband of
Mary, mother of Jesus. Joseph was a carpenter and
a devoted foster-father to Jesus. He took his family
to Egypt to escape the wrath of King Herod and
returned them to Jerusalem after Herod's death.
Veneration of Joseph in the West did not become
widespread until the fifteenth century. His feast day
is March 19, and he is considered a patron of car-
penters, workers, and social justice.

SAN MARTIN DE TOURS

Saint Martin of Tours (ca. 316–97) was born in Hungary to a pagan army officer. As a soldier stationed in Amiens, France, he famously cut his cloak in half to clothe a beggar in the freezing cold—thus the image represented in this *santo*. That night he had a vision of Christ in his half cloak. His shrine at Tours is one of the most popular for European pilgrims, and he is considered a patron of France. His feast day is November 11.

SAN MIGUEL

DENVER PUBLIC LIBRARY WESTERN HISTORY AND GENEALOGY DEPARTMENT

The archangel Michael is regarded as protector of the faithful against the devil and the helper of Christian armies against heathens. He led the good angels in a rout of Satan and his evil followers, who they drove out of heaven and into hell. San Miguel is seen here in his traditional pose, standing with a sword over a conquered Satan. His feast day is September 29.

SAN RAFAEL

DENVER PUBLIC LIBRARY WESTERN HISTORY AND GENEALOGY DEPARTMENT

Saint Rafael, one of seven archangels, is the patron of travelers, the blind, happy meetings, nurses, and physicians. His feast day is September 29.

SANTA BARBARA

Barbara is revered as a fourth-century virgin martyr,
though some historians doubt such a person existed.
According to legend, she resisted her pagan father's
demands that she marry, so he imprisoned her in
a tower, where she was tortured and condemned
to death. The site of her martyrdom was variously
described as Antioch, Heliopolis, Nicomedia, and
Rome. Barbara is the patron of architects and build-
ers, and her feast day is December 4. She is typically
portrayed, as here, with a building.

SANTA RITA

Rita of Cascia (1381–1457) was born near Spoleto,
Italy, and forced into marriage at age twelve. After
the death of her husband and two sons, she joined
the Augustinian order, where she became known
for her austerities, penances, and prayers to bring
others back to their religion. She is the patron of
desperate causes, and her feast day is May 22.

SEÑORA DE GUADALUPE

Denver Public Library Western History and Genealogy Department

Our Lady of Guadalupe, also known as the Virgin of Guadalupe, is Mexico's most popular and important religious and cultural image. On the morning of December 9, 1531, the Virgin Mary appeared to an Indian boy named Juan Diego on a hill near Mexico City and asked him to have a church built in her honor on the site. When asked for a sign to prove her identity, she healed Juan Diego's sick uncle, then produced out-of-season red Castilian roses, which she placed in the boy's cloak. When he related the story to his bishop, the flowers fell to the floor, revealing a miraculous image of the virgin on the fabric of his cloak. Our Lady of Guadalupe is revered as a patroness to the nation of Mexico. She is also a favorite with Hispanic Catholics in the southwestern United States.

THE ARCADE SALOON, DENVER

WATERCOLOR AND GOUACHE, 1941, DENVER PUBLIC
LIBRARY WESTERN HISTORY AND GENEALOGY
DEPARTMENT. PUBLISHED IN THE *ROCKY MOUNTAIN
NEWS*, MARCH 23, 1941.

This painting shows the old Arcade buildings at
1609–15 Larimer Street. The Arcade was a gambling
establishment and saloon, started by Ed Chase and
later owned by Vaso Chucovich. Chase presided
over his underworld domain from the Arcade,
hosting notorious characters such as Soapy Smith,
Deadeye Dick, and Bat Masterson. Like many elegant Denver landmarks, the Arcade fell to Denver's
Skyline Urban Renewal project in the 1970s. Its last
occupant was the Gold Nugget Bar & Grill. This
quintessential view of teh heart of Denver's Skid
Row includes two other fixtures: the Saint Vincent
de Paul Society's Salvage Bureau and one of the most
preeeminent rescue missions, the Citizens Mission.

FREDERICK J. BANCROFT FARM, DENVER

WATERCOLOR AND GOUACHE, 1941, DENVER PUBLIC LIBRARY WESTERN HISTORY AND GENEALOGY DEPARTMENT. PUBLISHED IN THE *ROCKY MOUNTAIN NEWS*, MAY 4, 1941.

This painting shows the Frederick J. Bancroft farmhouse at Sheridan Boulevard and Morrison Road in Denver, Colorado. Born in Enfield, Connecticut, Bancroft studied medicine at the University of Buffalo in 1861 and then joined the Union Army as a surgeon during the Civil War. He arrived in Denver in 1866 and soon provided a guiding force and influence for the development of both medicine and history in the new territory. He served as Arapahoe County physician (1866–69), Denver city physician (1872–76 and 1877–78), president of the Territorial Board of Health (1876), the first president of the State Board of Health (1877), and a founder of the University of Denver and Colorado Seminary Medical Department (1881). In addition, he helped found and presided over the State Historical and Natural History Society of Colorado, the forerunner of today's History Colorado, in 1879. His granddaughter, Caroline Bancroft, became a noted Colorado historian.

BARCLAY BLOCK, DENVER

WATERCOLOR AND GOUACHE, 1941, DENVER PUBLIC LIBRARY WESTERN HISTORY AND GENEALOGY DEPARTMENT. PUBLISHED IN THE *ROCKY MOUNTAIN NEWS*, APRIL 20, 1941.

The Barclay Hotel at 1751 Larimer Street in Denver was constructed in 1884 by the Denver Mansion Company, Ltd., a British investment house. Prior to completion of the state capitol building, the Barclay hosted the Colorado Legislature. The Barclay featured large, comfortable rooms on the top floors, a dining room, shops, and a common area where legislators could congregate. The basement housed elaborate marble baths with artesian water and an underground tunnel connecting the Barclay to the adjacent Windsor Hotel, which allowed the lawmakers to drink discreetly at the Windsor's elegant bar. The area declined with the legislature's move to the new capitol building in 1895, and the Barclay became a skid-row flophouse before meeting the Denver Urban Renewal Authority's wrecking ball.

MARGARET "MOLLY" BROWN HOUSE, DENVER

WATER COLOR AND GOUACHE, 1941, DENVER PUBLIC
LIBRARY WESTERN HISTORY AND GENEALOGY
DEPARTMENT. PUBLISHED IN THE *ROCKY MOUNTAIN
NEWS*, MAY 6, 1941.

The house at 1340 Pennsylvania Street in Capitol
Hill was designed by architect William Lang in
1889 for silver magnates Isaac and Mary Large.
Lang's unique combination of Classic Queen Anne,
Richardsonian Romanesque, and Neoclassical styles
made for an eclectic but elegant home design. Lang
created a rugged facade with rhyolite but incorporated stained glass windows, ornamental wood
panels, and round arch windows to create a softer,
luxurious feel. The silver crash resulting from the
repeal of the Sherman Silver Act hit the Larges hard,
leading them to sell the home to James Joseph "J.J."
Brown in April 1894.

In 1898 Brown transferred title of the house to
his wife, Margaret, who is better remembered by
the world as "the Unsinkable Molly Brown." When
the socialite, activist, and philanthropist traveled
abroad, she often rented the house to various
wealthy families. In 1902 the home became the
temporary residence of Governor James Orman and
his family. The Great Depression forced Margaret to
turn the home into a boardinghouse, and it was sold
following her death in 1932.

Subsequent owners altered the house, creating twelve separate units for renters. In 1958 Art
Leisenring purchased the house, at first running a
gentlemen's boardinghouse and then leasing it to
the city for use as a home for wayward girls. Seeing
the threat of demolition for this and other historic
Denver structures, Leisenring and a group of other
concerned citizens incorporated Historic Denver,
Inc., in 1970. The group's first grassroots campaign
sought to save the Molly Brown House from demolition. Through aggressive fundraising and media
appeals, Historic Denver, Inc., was able to purchase
and restore the Brown house based on photographs
from 1910. The Molly Brown House Museum is
now a major tourist attraction and an enduring
symbol of Gilded Age Denver and a remarkable
self-made woman.

WILLIAM BYERS HOME, DENVER

WATERCOLOR AND GOUACHE, 1941, DENVER PUBLIC LIBRARY WESTERN HISTORY AND GENEALOGY DEPARTMENT. PUBLISHED IN THE *ROCKY MOUNTAIN NEWS*, FEBRUARY 9, 1941.

This painting shows the now demolished William N. Byers home at 1800 South Sherman Street, in the Platte Park neighborhood. An early settler of Denver and the founder and editor of the *Rocky Mountain News*, Byers is more readily associated by the public with his residence at 1310 Bannock Street, which has been preserved by History Colorado as the Byers-Evans House, a museum popular with Coloradans and visitors alike. Byers became Denver's foremost publicist and promoter, even going so far as to claim that steamships could serve the city. He more realistically promoted the unification of onetime rivals Denver City and Auraria City in 1860 and construction of the Denver Pacific Railroad in 1870 to keep Denver alive by connecting it to the transcontinental railroad in Cheyenne.

CABLE CAR GARAGE, DENVER

WATERCOLOR AND GOUACHE, 1941, DENVER PUBLIC LIBRARY WESTERN HISTORY AND GENEALOGY DEPARTMENT. PUBLISHED IN THE *ROCKY MOUNTAIN NEWS*, JANUARY 12, 1941.

The Denver City Cable Railway Building at 1801 Lawrence Street opened in 1889 to house the power plant, car barn, garage, and repair shop for Denver's cable car system. This brick building was crafted by artisans and features intricate patterns, archways, and rounded brick detail. Added to the National Register of Historic Places in 1979, it has been restored to house a ground-floor restaurant, the popular and long-lived Old Spaghetti Factory, with a cable car to dine in and the longest bar in Denver.

CAMP WELD, DENVER

WATERCOLOR AND GOUACHE, 1941, DENVER PUBLIC LIBRARY WESTERN HISTORY AND GENEALOGY DEPARTMENT. PUBLISHED IN THE *ROCKY MOUNTAIN NEWS*, OCTOBER 20, 1940.

This cottage at West Eighth Avenue and Vallejo Street in Denver, which no longer stands, was part of a military installation known as Camp Weld, home base to the First Regiment of the Colorado Volunteer Infantry during the Civil War. The camp hosted a fateful conference on September 28, 1864, when Governor John Evans and Colonel John Chivington met with five chiefs, including Black Kettle of the Cheyenne and White Antelope of the Arapaho, who had come to Denver to parley for peace. The chiefs agreed to peacefully settle their people on the reservation at Sand Creek, about forty miles northwest of Fort Lyon, created by the Fort Wise Treaty of 1860. On November 29, Chivington and 700 soldiers of the Third Colorado Cavalry descended on the peaceful camp while most of its men of fighting age were away on a hunting expedition. Approximately 163 Cheyenne and Arapaho, mostly women, children, and elders, were killed in the ensuing Sand Creek Massacre.

CARLSBAD CAVERNS, NEW MEXICO

WATERCOLOR AND GOUACHE PAINTING, 1945, DENVER
PUBLIC LIBRARY WESTERN HISTORY AND GENEALOGY
DEPARTMENT.

The Carlsbad Caverns in Carlsbad Caverns
National Park in the Guadalupe Mountains of
southeastern New Mexico are among over 300
limestone caves in a fossil reef created by an inland
sea 250 million to 280 million years ago. The
largest "room" in the Carlsbad Caverns has an
area of 357,469 square feet and a height of 255 feet.
Native Americans living in the nearby Guadalupe
Mountains 12,000 to 14,000 years ago left picto-
graphs and evidence of cooking ring sites within
the present-day boundaries of the park.

Carlsbad Cave National Monument was
created in 1923 and became Carlsbad Caverns
National Park in 1930. The park has two historic
districts on the National Register of Historic
Places—the Cavern Historic District and the
Rattlesnake Springs Historic District. The park
museum and its archives contain more than
1 million cultural resource artifacts that are being
preserved for future study.

CHARPIOT'S HOTEL, DENVER

WATERCOLOR, 1940, DENVER PUBLIC LIBRARY WESTERN HISTORY AND GENEALOGY DEPARTMENT. PUBLISHED IN THE *ROCKY MOUNTAIN NEWS*, JULY 21, 1940.

In 1872 Fred Charpiot, a native of France who had been running a restaurant in Denver since 1867, opened the Charpiot Hotel and restaurant at 356 Larimer (later 1540 Larimer). The hotel became a favorite of European tourists and successful miners. In his 1880 book *History of the City of Denver*, author O. L. Baskin declared that "the reputation of the house and its owner has extended through this country and Europe, the house being the favorite resort of the best class of European tourists in Colorado, and many an old miner will long remember with what satisfaction, after the months of the frugal fare of a mining camp, he sat down to a 'square meal' at Charpiot's." By Herndon Davis's day, the fine hotel had given way to inexpensive residential apartments and store fronts, but the inscription atop the building still proudly proclaimed it the "Delmonico of the West."

EDWARD CHASE HOME, DENVER

WATERCOLOR AND GOUACHE, 1941, DENVER PUBLIC LIBRARY WESTERN HISTORY AND GENEALOGY DEPARTMENT. PUBLISHED IN THE *ROCKY MOUNTAIN NEWS*, MARCH 2, 1941.

This painting shows the now demolished Edward Chase residence at 2859 Lawrence Street, featuring a covered porch and balcony. Chase was a proprietor of gambling establishments with sometime partner Soapy Smith. After arriving in Denver in 1860, the handsome, blue-eyed Chase impressed many with his knowledge of games of chance. Jerome B. Chaffee, later a US senator, backed Chase when he decided to open his own gambling business. Chase owned the Progressive, the Palace, the Cricket Club, the Interocean Club, and the Navarre, among other "gambling hells" in downtown Denver. He became a "boss" of Denver's underworld and enjoyed a comfortable "business" relationship with Mayor Robert Speer, who shielded Chase's illegal operations from prosecution.

CITY HALL, DENVER

WATERCOLOR AND GOUACHE, 1941, DENVER PUBLIC LIBRARY WESTERN HISTORY AND GENEALOGY DEPARTMENT. PUBLISHED IN THE *ROCKY MOUNTAIN NEWS*, JANUARY 26, 1941.

This painting portrays the 1883 Denver City Hall, razed in 1937, at 14th and Larimer Streets. It was the scene of Denver's "City Hall War" of 1894. After the Populist Davis Hanson Waite's election as governor of Colorado in 1893, he set out to dismantle the corrupt political machine in Denver that was controlled by notorious operators such as Jefferson Randolph "Soapy" Smith. Waite fired Smith allies Jackson Orr and D. J. Martin from the Denver Fire and Police Board for refusing to enforce the gambling laws. They refused to leave their offices and barricaded themselves in the City Hall with 300 other anti-Waite officials and their supporters. Waite called in the

state militia, which was joined by federal troops. On March 15, 1894, they marched into Denver with cannon and Gatling guns and took up positions outside City Hall. The tense standoff continued until the Colorado Supreme Court agreed to take the case. Waite's appointees were eventually seated without violence. Soapy Smith's saloons were closed for gambling violations, and he left the state to pursue his criminal schemes in Skagway, Alaska. This building remained Denver's City Hall until the 1932 completion of the current City and County Building as a much larger city hall. The old City Hall bell on a pedestal marks the site of a demolished landmark today.

CITY HOTEL, SILVER PLUME, COLORADO

WATERCOLOR AND GOUACHE, 1940, DENVER PUBLIC
LIBRARY WESTERN HISTORY AND GENEALOGY
DEPARTMENT. PUBLISHED IN THE *ROCKY MOUNTAIN
NEWS*, OCTOBER 27, 1940.

This watercolor and gouache painting shows the
City Hotel in the Clear Creek County silver mining
town of Silver Plume, Colorado, featuring a second
story balcony and a high false front.

RUFUS "POTATO" CLARK HOME, DENVER

WATERCOLOR AND GOUACHE, 1941, DENVER PUBLIC LIBRARY WESTERN HISTORY AND GENEALOGY DEPARTMENT. PUBLISHED IN THE *ROCKY MOUNTAIN NEWS*, DECEMBER 22, 1940.

This watercolor painting portrays the now-demolished Rufus A. Clark house at 1395 South Cherokee Street in Denver's Platte Park neighborhood. Rufus "Potato" Clark, a Colorado pioneer, arrived from Iowa in July 1859 with his wife and child in an ox-pulled covered wagon. He staked out a large farm along the South Platte River across from Ruby Hill, the first parcel of his Colorado landholdings that eventually totaled 20,000 acres. Before settling down in the Denver area, Clark had experienced many adventures: he ran away from home and worked at sea for ten years, spent two years as a '49er mining gold in California, then

mined in Australia, once reportedly walking from Sydney to Melbourne—a distance of 400 miles.

Clark returned to the United States in 1854, took up farming, and started a family. His main product was potatoes, hence his nickname. He was known to be honest and generous, despite his fondness for hard drinking and profanity prior to a midlife religious conversion. Clark won election to the Legislative Assembly of the Territory of Colorado in 1864 and served on the Arapahoe County school board. He became a leading philanthropist and donated 80 acres for the campus of what is now the University of Denver.

E. A. COLBURN STABLES, DENVER

WATERCOLOR AND GOUACHE, 1941, DENVER PUBLIC LIBRARY WESTERN HISTORY AND GENEALOGY DEPARTMENT. PUBLISHED IN THE *ROCKY MOUNTAIN NEWS*, FEBRUARY 2, 1941.

This painting shows Judge Earnest A. Colburn's former horse stables at 1500 South Broadway, in Denver's Platte Park neighborhood. The two-story building and barn feature hip roofs and signs: "Used Furniture Antiques, We Buy Anything." Judge Colburn made a fortune as owner of the Dubuque Mining and Tunnel Company in the Cripple Creek mining district. He backed his sons, Herbert C. Colburn and Earnest A. Colburn Jr., in the Colburn Automobile Company, which manufactured "horseless carriages" in Denver from 1906 to 1911. These structures became the hub of today's Antique Row.

JOHN L. DAILEY MANSION, DENVER

WATERCOLOR AND GOUACHE, 1940, DENVER PUBLIC LIBRARY WESTERN HISTORY AND GENEALOGY DEPARTMENT. PUBLISHED IN THE *ROCKY MOUNTAIN NEWS*, DECEMBER 1, 1940.

The John L. Dailey house at Fourth and Broadway in Denver, Colorado, was a two-story brick structure with a covered porch, balcony, and rusticated stone base. A native of Seneca County, Ohio, Dailey learned the printer's trade in Indiana, Nebraska, and South Dakota before moving to Denver in the spring of 1859 with the William N. Byers party. With their Omaha printing press, they produced the first issue of the *Rocky Mountain News* on April 23, 1859. While Byers was doing promotion and traveling, Dailey did much of the work of running the newspaper. Dailey sold his interest in the *Rocky* to Byers on October 31, 1870, for $6,000. The following year, Dailey partnered with Nathan A.

Baker and Charles W. Smart to form the printing company Dailey, Baker and Smart. They brought the first steam-powered printing plant to Denver and gained control of the *Denver Daily Times* in June 1872, which they sold to Frederick J. Stanton in July 1875. Dailey served as Arapahoe County treasurer from 1877 to 1883 and became a member and the first president of the Denver Board of Park Commissioners. John L. Dailey and his brother, William M. Dailey, established Dailey and Company, a real estate and loan concern, in the 1880s. Dailey died in Denver on January 3, 1908. Dailey Park at West Ellsworth Avenue and Cherokee Street is named for him.

DENVER POST BUILDING, DENVER

WATERCOLOR AND GOUACHE PAINTING, 1948, DENVER PUBLIC LIBRARY WESTERN HISTORY AND GENEALOGY DEPARTMENT

This four-story building at 1544 Champa Street housed the *Denver Post* from 1907 to 1950. It carried the slogan "O Justice When Expelled from Other Habitations, Make This Thy Dwelling Place" and had a large tin rooftop statue of a blindfolded justice with her scales. With incessant promotions ranging from circus acts to tossing silver dollars down into the crowd to an electric signboard with the latest news and sports scores, Frederick G. Bonfils and Henry H. Tammen made the *Post* a frequent attraction for crowds. This now-demolished downtown landmark was one of Herndon Davis's workplaces for many years.

DENVER PRESS CLUB MURAL

CA. 1945

As an illustrator for both the *Rocky Mountain News* and the *Denver Post*—and an avid drinker—Davis frequented the Denver Press Club at 1330 Glenarm Place in Denver. Founded in 1867, the Denver Press Club claims to be the oldest press club in the United States. Early meetings were held in the basement of Wolfe Londoner's grocery store on Larimer Street; later, the club held court at a variety of Denver hotels, including the prestigious Brown Palace. In addition to enjoying drink, poker, and camaraderie, club members brought in national journalists, performers, orators, and other celebrities. In 1925 the club built this home on Glenarm Place. Designed by prominent Colorado architects Burnham and Merrill Hoyt, the building features meal and bar service on its main level, a large meeting and banquet facility

on the second floor, and a basement with a billiards room and a card room. It has hosted regular poker games since the day the club opened. In 1986 the Denver Press Club gained designation as a Denver Historic Landmark. The Society for Professional Journalists designated the club a "significant historical place in journalism" in 2008.

Herndon Davis graced the basement card room with this mural in 1945. It depicts the bustling Press Room of the *Rocky Mountain News*, a place Davis knew well. Denver journalism luminaries immortalized in the mural include *News* columnist Lew Casey, editor and *Denver Business Journal* founder Gene Cervi, *News* City Room chief Bob Chase, *Post* journalist and author Gene Fowler, and *News* photographer Harry Rhoads.

ELDORADO HOTEL, DENVER

WATERCOLOR AND GOUACHE, 1941, DENVER PUBLIC LIBRARY WESTERN HISTORY AND GENEALOGY DEPARTMENT.
PUBLISHED IN THE *ROCKY MOUNTAIN NEWS*, FEBRUARY 23, 1941.

Built by Henri and Katrina Murat, this log build-ing at 1249 10th Street (near Larimer) was the first hotel in the Denver area. Assisted by David Smoke, Count Henri Murat built a twenty- by seventeen-foot cabin made of hewn cottonwood logs with a dirt floor and gave it the impressive name "Eldorado Hotel." Despite the primitive accommodations, Katrina's cooking and hospital-ity won over guests. Travelers who stayed at the Eldorado enjoyed her home-cooked meals, fol-lowed by apple strudels for dessert. Katrina sewed her Parisian undergarments into the first US flag in Denver, which the Murats proudly flew over their hotel.

JOHN ELSNER OFFICE BUILDING, DENVER

WATERCOLOR AND GOUACHE, 1941, DENVER PUBLIC LIBRARY WESTERN HISTORY AND GENEALOGY DEPARTMENT. PUBLISHED IN THE *ROCKY MOUNTAIN NEWS*, OCTOBER 6, 1940.

The building at 1321 Curtis Street served as both the home and medical office of Dr. John Elsner, a leading pioneer Denver physician. Born in Vienna in 1844, Elsner studied at Bellevue Medical College in New York. In addition to medicine, Elsner studied mineralogy, becoming an expert in the classification of stones and minerals. In 1866 he joined a wagon train, walking or riding horseback all the way to the Colorado Territory. He set up a medical practice in Denver, distributing circulars

with the *Rocky Mountain News* to attract business. Elsner created the first Arapahoe County Hospital in a small shelter at 9th and Mariposa Streets and was appointed county physician in 1870. He was also active in Denver's Jewish community, helping to found Congregation Emmanuel in 1872 and serving as president of the Denver Lodge of B'nai B'rith in 1874. In 1889 Dr. Elsner helped establish National Jewish Hospital and served on the board of trustees.

EMMANUEL-SHERITH CHAPEL/ SYNAGOGUE, DENVER

WATERCOLOR AND GOUACHE, 1940, DENVER PUBLIC
LIBRARY WESTERN HISTORY AND GENEALOGY
DEPARTMENT. PUBLISHED IN THE *ROCKY MOUNTAIN
NEWS*, DECEMBER 8, 1940.

This painting shows the Emmanuel-Sherith Chapel/
Synagogue at 1201 10th Street and the corner of
Lawrence Street in Denver's Auraria neighborhood.
Built in 1877 as Emmanuel Episcopal Chapel, this
rhyolite Gothic revival style structure is the oldest
surviving church building in Denver. In 1903 it was
purchased by East European Jews moving into the
West Colfax Avenue neighborhood sometimes called
"Little Israel." The new owners added the Hebrew
inscription over the entry and the Star of David atop
the building, which they renamed the Congregation
Sherith Israel. After that synagogue closed in 1958,
it became a studio for artist Wolfgang Pogzeba.
Since the 1970s, it has served as a student art gallery
on the Auraria Higher Education Center campus.
The restored structure is on the National Register
of Historic Places and was designated Denver
Landmark #1 in 1968.

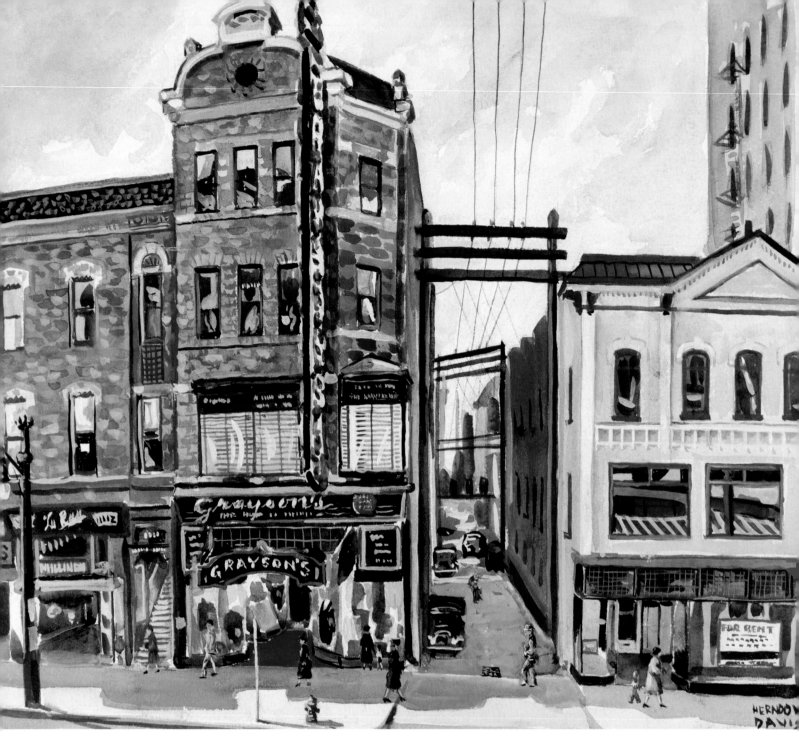

EUGENE FIELD ALLEY, DENVER

WATERCOLOR AND GOUACHE, 1940, DENVER PUBLIC LIBRARY WESTERN HISTORY AND GENEALOGY DEPARTMENT. PUBLISHED IN THE *ROCKY MOUNTAIN NEWS*, NOVEMBER 17, 1940.

This alley between 15th, 16th, Lawrence, and Arapahoe Streets, flanked by office buildings and storefronts, took its nickname from Eugene Field, writer and editor of the *Denver Tribune* from 1881 to 1884. According to Robert Perkins, author of *The First Hundred Years: An Informal History of Denver and the Rocky Mountain News*, Field was a "legend" as editor of the *Tribune*, a "jackanapes and pungent paragrapher," who lost no opportunity to send a barbed dart, taking on "the rest of the local press, politicians of both stripes, and any likely businessman." Field is best known for his poems for children, including *Wynken, Blynken, and Nod*. The alley was also called "Newspaper Alley."

WILLIAM GARRETT FISHER MANSION, DENVER

WATERCOLOR AND GOUACHE, 1940, DENVER PUBLIC LIBRARY WESTERN HISTORY AND GENEALOGY DEPARTMENT. PUBLISHED IN THE *ROCKY MOUNTAIN NEWS*, SEPTEMBER 22, 1940.

This painting portrays the William Garrett Fisher Mansion at 1600 Logan Street in the North Capitol Hill neighborhood. Prominent Denver architect Frank Edbrooke constructed the neoclassic residence in 1896 for William Garrett Fisher, partner in the Daniels and Fisher Department Store. The William Garrett Fisher Mansion features massive two-story columns supporting an entry portico. The walls of the flat-roofed residence are of polished stone, with carved stone panels embellishing the third level. Around 1900, a one-story wing on the north was added for Fisher's widow, creating space for a ballroom and an art gallery. The William Garrett Fisher Mansion was added to the National Register of Historic Places in 1974. Architect David O. Tryba purchased the property in 1999, rehabilitating it for use as his firm's office and his family residence.

FORT GARLAND, COLORADO

PAINTING, HISTORY COLORADO

Fort Garland, located in Costilla County in southern Colorado, was built in 1858 to house soldiers protecting settlers in the San Luis Valley. It replaced nearby Fort Massachusetts (1852–58), which was abandoned because of its poor location. The new fort, named for General John Garland, commander of the Military District of New Mexico, initially policed Ute Indians. During the Civil War, troops from Fort Garland marched south to bolster Union forces facing a Confederate invasion aimed at capturing the Colorado goldfields. Victory by the First Colorado Infantry and units of the First and Third US Cavalry at Glorieta Pass in March 1862 saved the West for the Union. After the war, Colonel Kit Carson led a unit of New Mexico volunteers stationed at Fort Garland. Carson succeeded in negotiating a treaty with the Utes and kept the San Luis Valley relatively peaceful.

The Ninth Cavalry, made up of the storied African American Buffalo Soldiers, was stationed at Fort Garland between 1876 and 1879. These troops were called to the La Plata region and to the Ute Reservation to prevent conflict between the Utes and white prospectors. Following the Meeker Massacre at the White River Agency in 1879, Fort Garland's garrison was enlarged, and the fort served as a base of operations against Indians. With the removal of the Utes to Utah, the fort was no longer needed and was officially abandoned in 1883.

The Colorado Historical Society (now History Colorado) restored the fort and turned it into the Fort Garland Museum in 1950. The museum features restored and reconstructed buildings, including the adobe Commandant's Quarters, where Kit Carson and his wife once lived, and cavalry barracks with exhibits of Hispanic traditional arts.

FORT GARLAND COMMANDANT'S QUARTERS

PEN DRAWING, DENVER PUBLIC LIBRARY WESTERN HISTORY AND GENEALOGY DEPARTMENT

This undated work shows the door to Fort Garland's Commandant's Quarters, where Christopher "Kit" Carson and other US Army officers stayed. The style of the drawing harks back to the cross-line technique that won Davis critical acclaim early in his career. These quarters and Fort Garland have been restored as a museum by History Colorado in the tiny town of Fort Garland.

FOUR MILE HOUSE, DENVER

OIL PAINTING, 1940, DENVER PUBLIC LIBRARY WESTERN HISTORY AND GENEALOGY DEPARTMENT

The Four Mile House was built on the banks of Cherry Creek in 1859. Beginning in 1860, it served as a last stop for travelers coming west along the Cherokee Trail prior to reaching Denver. One of a string of mile houses along Cherry Creek, it is four miles from downtown Denver. It was operated by the widow Mary Cawker from 1860 to 1864, then by new owners Levi and Mille Booth. The Booths bought surrounding property and built a thriving farm while continuing to offer hospitality to travelers. The arrival of railroads in 1870 reduced stage and freight business, but the Booth family continued to live and work on the property until the 1940s. Honey was one of their biggest products;

at one time the Booth's farm had enough bee hives to produce 4,000 pounds of honey in a single year.

In 1975 the City of Denver bought the house at 715 South Forest Street and East Exposition Avenue and the remaining 12 acres of the farm, turning the property into a Denver City Park. The Four Mile House was restored and the park opened to the public in 1978. Although city-owned, it is operated as a living history park and museum by the nonprofit Four Mile Historic Park, Inc. It is a Denver Historic Landmark and was listed on the National Register of Historic Places in 1969. Visitors to Four Mile Historic Park can tour the oldest structure in Denver and learn about nineteenth-century frontier farming.

HERNDON
DAVIS
1940

GLOBEVILLE SMELTER, GLOBEVILLE, COLORADO

WATERCOLOR, 1940, DENVER PUBLIC LIBRARY WESTERN HISTORY AND GENEALOGY DEPARTMENT. PUBLISHED IN THE *ROCKY MOUNTAIN NEWS*, JULY 14, 1940.

The Globeville neighborhood of Denver is home to the historic Globe Smelter at East 51st Avenue and Washington Street. It was originally known as the Holden Smelter, for entrepreneur Edward R. Holden, who built it in 1886. The refining of ores was crucial to the early economies of both Colorado and Denver. Indeed, Denver historian Jerome C. Smiley asserted in 1901 that the smelters' "economic value to the city of Denver far exceeds that of any other industry; indeed, it may be said that it overshadows that of all other industries."

The Holden Smelter refined silver and lead. When the heavily leveraged Holden defaulted on loans, Colorado National Bank stepped in and appointed Dennis Sheedy manager. He reorganized the operation as the Globe Smelting and Refining

Company in January 1889, and the small neighborhood surrounding the smelter came to be known as "Globeville." Initially a separate town, it was annexed to Denver in 1902. In 1899 the Globe was absorbed into the American Smelting and Refining Company (ASARCO). The smelter prospered during World War I, but depleted ore resources and changed market conditions caused the Globe to switch to producing cadmium, an element used as a protective coating for aircraft during World War II. In 1993 the firm shifted to a focus on the development of specialty metals, such as bismuth. That same year, a group of residents won a lawsuit against ASARCO alleging air, soil, and groundwater pollution. The courts ordered the company to pay for soil remediation in Globeville in 1997, and it shut down in 2006.

GOVERNOR'S MANSION, DENVER

WATERCOLOR, 1961, DENVER PUBLIC LIBRARY WESTERN HISTORY AND GENEALOGY DEPARTMENT

The Colorado Governor's Mansion at 400 East 8th Avenue in Denver was designed by architects Marean and Norton as a palatial residence for Walter Scott Cheesman, an early Denver booster who helped bring railroad service to the city and developed its fledgling real estate industry and who also headed the Denver Union Water Company. His daughter Gladys helped him plan the home, but Walter Cheesman died in 1907, before construction had begun. His daughter and his widow, Alice, proceeded with the plans. The elegant three-story home they built featured a wrought iron fence, a west portico with a two-story Roman Ionic colonnade, a widow's walk, and graceful arched windows. The Cheesman home became the envy of Denver society.

In 1908 Gladys married John Evans, grandson of the second territorial governor of Colorado, and the house was completed the same year. The Evans family added new features over time, including a rose garden, a lily pool with pergola, and a solarium constructed in 1915. When Mrs. Cheesman died in 1923, prominent businessman Claude K. Boettcher purchased the home. He gave the deed to his wife, Edna, as a Valentine's Day present in 1924. The Boettchers traveled the world acquiring furnishings and works of art, many of which still belong to the modern mansion collection. They added two small wings to the Palm Room and remodeled the upstairs bedroom suites.

Claude Boettcher died in 1957 and his wife died the following year. She left the elegant mansion to the Boettcher Foundation, requesting that it be offered to the State of Colorado as a governor's residence. The gift was rejected by several state agencies, and the house faced the wrecking ball until late 1959, when Governor Stephen McNichols stepped in to accept the hilltop mansion on behalf of the state. The mansion is listed on the National Register of Historic Places and is a Denver Historic Landmark. It is open for free tours.

KATE HALLACK HOME, DENVER

WATERCOLOR AND GOUACHE, 1940, DENVER PUBLIC LIBRARY WESTERN HISTORY AND GENEALOGY DEPARTMENT. PUBLISHED IN THE *ROCKY MOUNTAIN NEWS*, DECEMBER 15, 1940.

The Kate Hallack residence at East 17th Avenue and Sherman Streets was built by Erastus F. Hallack for his bride, Kate Gray, of Bethany, New York. Erastus Hallack was a lumber baron who, along with his brother Charles, created the Hallack Brothers Lumber Company. This Queen Anne style mansion showcased various fine woods obtained by the lumber company. The house met the wrecking ball in 1941. The site is now occupied by Denver's most notable highrise, the Wells Fargo Tower, popularly known as the Cash Register Building.

GRAVES OF "WILD BILL" HICKOK AND MARTHA "CALAMITY JANE" CANARY BURKE, DEADWOOD, SOUTH DAKOTA

WATERCOLOR AND GOUACHE, 1946, DENVER PUBLIC LIBRARY WESTERN HISTORY AND GENEALOGY DEPARTMENT

Famous Old West figures "Wild Bill" Hickok and "Calamity Jane" Canary Burke are buried next to one another in Mount Moriah Cemetery near Deadwood, South Dakota. A monument honoring Hickok was built near the grave. Calamity Jane's dying wish was to be buried next to Hickok, who reportedly "had no use" for her. However, the men of the self-appointed committee who planned Calamity Jane's funeral—Albert Malter, Frank Ankeney, Jim Carson, and Anson Higby—decided to play a posthumous joke on Hickok by laying her to rest by his side.

JOHN B. HINDRY HOUSE, DENVER

WATERCOLOR, 1940, DENVER PUBLIC LIBRARY WESTERN HISTORY AND GENEALOGY DEPARTMENT. PUBLISHED IN THE *ROCKY MOUNTAIN NEWS*, JULY 7, 1940.

This watercolor painting shows the John B. Hindry residence at 5500 Washington Street in Denver. The home featured a tall cupola, quoins, bay window, portico, and elaborate cornices. Hindry was a builder and contractor from New York who was active in Denver in the 1890s. Hindry and his house became notorious for the booby traps he set, which killed two intruders and finally injured Hindry himself.

With profits from his sawmill in Bear Creek Canyon, Hindry purchased 110 acres of land on the Platte River in 1870, where he planned to build an exclusive subdivision. His own home was built in 1873 on the highest point of land in the area. His Italianate showpiece was two-and-a-half stories tall, with two iron lions guarding the entrance. The ten-room interior featured black walnut panels and Italian marble. Hindry built a two-story brick stable where he kept fine trotting horses, a schoolhouse for his children, and a greenhouse with surrounding landscaping. But his dream house turned into a nightmare when the Holden Smelter, later known as the Globe Smelter, began operating a short distance upriver from the house. The smelter's foul smoke and fumes killed plant life on Hindry's estate, making it difficult to keep horses because their pasture had died. The smelter also killed his hopes for an attractive subdivision.

With his children grown and his wife deceased, rumors began to circulate that Hindry was a miser with a great treasure in gold hoarded in his house of broken dreams. Thieves began to prowl the property, lured by the stories of treasure. In response, Hindry rigged a booby trap with a shotgun aimed at the only window easily accessible from outside. Hindry's trap claimed its first victim on September 18, 1901; two more would-be intruders met the same fate. Each death brought questions from the authorities but no charges. While sleeping one night, Hindry thought he heard prowlers and went downstairs to investigate. Entering the room containing the trap, he tripped over the trigger cord and was shot in the right side. He lay injured for three days without help until he mustered the strength to saddle a horse and ride to a doctor. Defeated in his attempts to sue the smelter owners and never having fully recovered his health after the shooting, Hindry moved to California, where he died in 1906.

The house stood vacant and gained a reputation for being haunted. It was eventually purchased at tax sale and used for a variety of purposes: as a spaghetti restaurant, an isolation hospital, and then again as a residence with a packing plant and market on the premises. The house burned in 1968 and was razed.

HOLYOKE, COLORADO, TRAIN TIME

WATERCOLOR AND GOUACHE, 1961, DENVER PUBLIC LIBRARY WESTERN HISTORY AND GENEALOGY DEPARTMENT

This painting portrays a Chicago, Burlington and Quincy train arriving at Holyoke, the largest town and county seat of Phillips County, Colorado.

HOTEL DE PARIS, GEORGETOWN, COLORADO

WATERCOLOR, 1940, DENVER PUBLIC LIBRARY WESTERN HISTORY AND GENEALOGY DEPARTMENT. PUBLISHED IN THE *ROCKY MOUNTAIN NEWS*, NOVEMBER 3, 1940.

The Hotel de Paris in Clear Creek County was founded by Adolphe Francois Gerard, a Frenchman who spent time in Paris and New York before enlisting in the US Army and deserting in Wyoming. After changing his name to Louis Dupuy, he went to work for the *Rocky Mountain News* in 1869 as a reporter in the mining camps. Drawn by the promise of riches, Dupuy became a miner himself and was injured while saving a co-worker from an explosion in a mine above Georgetown and Silver Plume in 1873. Unable to continue mining, Dupuy was helped by the people of Georgetown, who raised enough money to rent the former Delmonico Bakery for him. Within a few years he was able to buy it, creating a restaurant and hotel called the Hotel de Paris. He expanded the building by the

early 1890s, adding numerous rooms, a large restaurant, a sizable kitchen, and an apartment for himself. Electric lighting replaced gas lamps in 1893. Dinners were served with elegant linens and imported glassware, and the menu included steaks from cattle raised on Dupuy's ranch in North Park.

Dupuy died of pneumonia on October 7, 1900, at age fifty-six. He left the hotel to his housekeeper, Sophie Gally, who died just four months after Dupuy. The hotel was purchased by the Burkholder family, who owned it until 1954, when the National Society of Colonial Dames of America in Colorado acquired it and turned it into a museum. The building was placed on the National Register of Historic Places in 1970. In 2012 the National Trust for Historic Preservation designated the hotel its only Rocky Mountain regional site, elevating its stature as a museum.

LAMONT SCHOOL OF MUSIC, DENVER

WATERCOLOR, DENVER PUBLIC LIBRARY WESTERN
HISTORY AND GENEALOGY DEPARTMENT

Founded in 1924 by renowned voice teacher
Florence Lamont Hinman, the Lamont School of
Music began as a private school in a home at 1170
Sherman Street. Under Hinman's direction, the
school flourished, becoming an important part of
Denver's cultural life in the 1920s and 1930s. In 1941
the school merged with the University of Denver
and moved into the now demolished former home
of John Sidney Brown at 909 Grant Street. The
Brown house is pictured in this undated watercolor
by Herndon Davis. It was demolished in 1968. The
Lamont School of Music, now on the University
of Denver's campus, remains a premier university
music performance school with a long-standing
tradition of excellence.

LINDELL HOTEL, DENVER

WATERCOLOR AND GOUACHE, 1940, DENVER PUBLIC LIBRARY WESTERN HISTORY AND GENEALOGY DEPARTMENT. PUBLISHED IN THE *ROCKY MOUNTAIN NEWS*, SEPTEMBER 8, 1940.

This painting shows a rooming house, formerly known as the West Lindell Hotel, at 11th and Larimer Streets in the Auraria neighborhood near the southwest bank of Cherry Creek. The hotel, built in 1878, featured a rooftop observatory. It incorporated an earlier structure on the site. The hotel survived until the 1970s, when the Denver Urban Renewal Authority leveled the area to build the Auraria Higher Education Center.

LITTLETON MILL, LITTLETON

WATERCOLOR AND GOUACHE, 1940, DENVER PUBLIC LIBRARY WESTERN HISTORY AND GENEALOGY DEPARTMENT. PUBLISHED IN THE *ROCKY MOUNTAIN NEWS*, SEPTEMBER 15, 1940.

The Littleton Flour Mill (formerly the Rough and Ready Flour Mill), at 5798 South Rapp Street, was one of Littleton's oldest and most historic buildings. Built in 1872 on land homesteaded by Littleton founder Richard Little, it served as a grain elevator as well as the Rough and Ready Flour Mill, owned by Little. The Denver and Rio Grande Railroad ran a spur line to the elevators and the mercantile thrived, shipping more than 64,000 bushels of wheat in 1921. The Rough and Ready Flour Mill burned down in 1959.

MONTANA CITY (DENVER, 1858)

WATERCOLOR AND GOUACHE, 1940, DENVER PUBLIC LIBRARY WESTERN HISTORY AND GENEALOGY DEPARTMENT. PUBLISHED IN THE *ROCKY MOUNTAIN NEWS*, DECEMBER 29, 1940.

Erected by the Denver Chapter of the Sons of the American Revolution in 1924, this monument stood by the South Platte River between Evans and Iliff Avenues, in Denver's Overland neighborhood. It commemorated Montana City, the first settlement in what was to become Denver, Colorado. Montana City was established on the east bank of the South Platte River and north of the confluence with Little Dry Creek, adjacent to placer gold diggings on the Platte. The site was soon abandoned in favor of Auraria, a few miles downstream at the confluence of the South Platte and Cherry Creek.

MOUNT MORRISON INCLINE RAILROAD, MORRISON, COLORADO

WATERCOLOR AND GOUACHE, 1961, DENVER PUBLIC LIBRARY WESTERN HISTORY AND GENEALOGY DEPARTMENT. ILLUSTRATION CREATED FOR *HISTORY OF RED ROCKS PARK AND THEATER* BY NOLIE MUMEY.

Red Rocks Park owner and promoter John Brisben Walker built this tourist attraction, which operated from 1909 until 1915 and promised a five-minute, two-mile round-trip for a dollar. The spectacular ride to the top of Mount Morrison offered a view of Red Rocks and Denver in the distance. The scar on the mountainside is now a hiking trail.

THE NAVARRE, DENVER

WATERCOLOR AND GOUACHE, 1947, DENVER PUBLIC LIBRARY WESTERN HISTORY AND GENEALOGY DEPARTMENT. PUBLISHED IN THE *ROCKY MOUNTAIN NEWS*, SEPTEMBER 29, 1940.

The Navarre Building, 1727 Tremont Place, is a storied gem in Denver's history. Designed by architect Frank E. Edbrooke and built in 1880, the elegant Italianate building opened as Brinker Collegiate Institute, a school for young women. When Joseph Brinker died in 1889, the building changed hands and reopened as Hotel Richelieu, a bordello. Legend has it that a tunnel in the Navarre cellar was constructed as the Brown Palace Hotel was being built in 1892, as a way to allow hotel guests to discretely visit the Richelieu. Later supposedly lost in a poker game, the building was renamed the Navarre after Henry of Navarre, the French king who loved high living. The Navarre became known as a respectable, high-end dining club, although illicit activity supposedly continued behind closed doors.

In the late 1940s Johnny Ott restored the Navarre's Victorian motif, refurbished the worn bar and booths, and turned the Navarre into one of Denver's finest dining establishments. Jazz clarinetist Peanuts Hucko, a veteran of Benny Goodman's and Louis Armstrong's big bands, reopened the Navarre for dining and musical entertainment in the late 1960s. The building changed hands several more times until 1997, when it was acquired by the Anschutz Corporation. Restored and refurbished, it became home to the American Museum of Western Art, which houses the finest private collection of US western art, the Anschutz Collection. The Navarre is a Denver Historic Landmark and is on the National Register of Historic Places. It is the oldest building in the city's central business district.

PALACE VARIETY THEATER AND GAMBLING PARLOR, DENVER

WATERCOLOR, 1940, DENVER PUBLIC LIBRARY WESTERN HISTORY AND GENEALOGY DEPARTMENT. PUBLISHED IN THE *ROCKY MOUNTAIN NEWS*, JULY 28, 1940.

This watercolor shows storefronts on Blake Street, originally occupied by the Palace Variety Theater and Gambling Parlor. Owned by Denver underworld titans "Big Ed" Chase and later Bat Masterson, the two-story building housed a theater that seated 750, with gambling rooms that could accommodate 200 more. The theater featured mostly "leg art," with girls waiting tables and doubling as stage performers or commercial companions. An 1880 showbill promised "A Palace of Real Pleasure and Voluptuous Art, where women fascinate the heart." The very Reverend Martin Hart of St. John's Episcopal Cathedral had a different opinion, calling the palace "a death-trap to young men, a foul den of vice and corruption." There were at least three murders on the premises in the 1870s and 1880s. By the time Herndon Davis painted it in 1940, the building was home to a hardware store. During the 1980s, the Palace Lofts were constructed on the site.

RICHARD PEARCE MANSION, DENVER

WATERCOLOR AND GOUACHE, 1941, DENVER PUBLIC LIBRARY WESTERN HISTORY AND GENEALOGY DEPARTMENT. PUBLISHED IN THE *ROCKY MOUNTAIN NEWS*, JANUARY 19, 1941.

This painting shows the Richard Pearce home at 1712 Sherman Street in the Capitol Hill neighborhood. Pearce, a metallurgist for the Boston and Colorado Smelting Company, made his fortune by discovering a more economical method of separating copper from gold. Pearce's innovations saved his employers a fortune by making it possible to process ore locally, eliminating the expense of sending it to specially equipped plants back East. His Queen Anne mansion had become a political clubhouse in Herndon Davis's day, as evidenced by the script reading "Democratic Club" over the door.

PULLMAN HOMESTEAD, GOLDEN, COLORADO

WATERCOLOR AND GOUACHE, 1940, DENVER PUBLIC
LIBRARY WESTERN HISTORY AND GENEALOGY
DEPARTMENT. PUBLISHED IN THE *ROCKY MOUNTAIN
NEWS*, NOVEMBER 24, 1940.

The George Mortimer Pullman house near Golden,
Colorado, was built in 1860 by George Pullman,
an engineer, entrepreneur, and industrialist. He
is best known for designing and manufacturing
the Pullman sleeping car, which revolutionized
American train travel. He started his fortune in the
1859 Pikes Peak Gold Rush by providing goods
and services to fortune seekers. His firm operated
a freight business and an ore-crushing mill and
accumulated 1,600 acres of real estate near Golden,
which was platted as Cold Spring Ranch. The ranch
became a prominent base camp for the goldfields,
where miners could purchase supplies, buy a meal
and a drink, and spend the night. It became known
as Pullman's Switch, where miners could exchange
weary teams of pack animals for fresh teams before
taking on the challenging mountain passes. The
bedding Pullman designed and built for miners
supposedly helped perfect his Pullman sleeper cars.
Pullman's house, painted bright orange as Davis has
it, was disassembled in 1965. Golden Landmarks
hopes to restore it someday.

RED ROCKS PARK SEAT OF PLUTO, ROCK OF CRONUS, ROCK FORMATIONS, MORRISON, COLORADO
WATERCOLOR, 1961, DENVER PUBLIC LIBRARY WESTERN HISTORY AND GENEALOGY DEPARTMENT

Red Rocks Park in Morrison, Colorado, was created from a natural amphitheater belonging to the
Fountain Formation, a set of red sandstone beds.
The idyllic spot was most likely used by the Utes
in earlier times, perhaps for their ceremonies. The
place was known to settlers as "Garden of the
Angels" and later as "Garden of the Titans," though
the folk name "Red Rocks" stuck to it as well.
Industrialist and publisher John Brisben Walker
noted the perfect acoustics and picturesque setting

of Red Rocks and bought the place with proceeds
from the sale of his *Cosmopolitan* magazine in 1906.
He produced the first series of concerts there, beginning in 1906. The celebrated operatic soprano Mary
Garden performed at Red Rocks on May 10, 1911,
and called it the finest venue at which she had ever
performed. Nolie Mumey, a Denver physician and
historian, commissioned Davis to illustrate his
booklet *History of Red Rocks Park and Theater*. Many
of the resulting eighteen images are reproduced

in this book. Those images (now in the Denver Public Library Western History and Genealogy Department) include those of John Brisben Walker, Arthur Lakes, Diplodocus, Stegosaurus, Trachodon, Deinotherium, William F. Cody, Nellie Melba, Mary Garden, Mount Morrison Incline, Rock of Cronus, Seat of Pluto, John Ross, Saul Caston, and Benjamin F. Stapleton.

George Cranmer, manager of Denver Parks, convinced the City of Denver to purchase the Red Rocks area from Walker in 1928. When the Great Depression brought New Deal funds to Colorado, Cranmer persuaded Denver mayor Benjamin

Franklin Stapleton to use the labor and resources of the Civilian Conservation Corps and the Works Progress Administration to transform Red Rocks into a modern performing venue. Construction began in 1936, and the amphitheater was completed in 1941. Red Rocks has hosted regular concert seasons every year since 1947. The Beatles played Red Rocks on August 26, 1964—their only concert on that US tour that did not sell out. Red Rocks has grown more popular as a performing venue with the passage of time and now hosts an ever broader spectrum of events. It has been rated repeatedly as one of America's top outdoor venues.

BARON WALTER VON RICHTHOFEN CASTLE, DENVER

WATERCOLOR, 1940, DENVER PUBLIC LIBRARY WESTERN HISTORY AND GENEALOGY DEPARTMENT. PUBLISHED IN THE *ROCKY MOUNTAIN NEWS*, AUGUST 18, 1940.

The Richthofen Castle at 7020 East 12th Avenue, in the Montclair neighborhood of Denver, was built by Baron Walter von Richthofen, a German immigrant. He employed architect Alexander Cazin to design the castle, which was completed in 1887. Later owners had architects Maurice B. Biscoe, Henry H. Hewitt, and Jacques Jules Benedict add to and remodel the Romanesque Revival rhyolite castle. Von Richthofen planned his castle as a showpiece for a new upscale residential subdivision called Montclair,

five miles east of downtown Denver. Annexed to Denver in 1902, the area remained mostly undeveloped until after World War II. The 15,000-square-foot Richthofen Castle has eight bedrooms, seven bathrooms, five fireplaces, a bar, drawing room, library, servants' quarters, butler's pantry, and billiards room. The unique home is a Denver Historic Landmark and was added to the National Register of Historic Places in 1974. The latest owners are restoring the castle and its adjacent gatehouse.

JENNIE ROGERS MANSION AKA "HOUSE OF MIRRORS," DENVER

WATERCOLOR AND GOUACHE, 1941, DENVER PUBLIC LIBRARY WESTERN HISTORY AND GENEALOGY DEPARTMENT. PUBLISHED IN THE *ROCKY MOUNTAIN NEWS*, MAY 4, 1941.

Jennie Rogers had this home built as a luxurious house of prostitution. The house attracted the envy of her rival madam Mattie Silks, who eventually bought it from Jennie. After reformers closed down the Market Street red light district in 1912, 1942 Market Street was rented by Japanese and converted to the Tri-State Buddhist Church. Later converted to a warehouse, it has been restored as a special events center.

RUSSELL GULCH, COLORADO—BARROOM BRAWL

WATERCOLOR AND GOUACHE, UNKNOWN DATE, DENVER PUBLIC LIBRARY WESTERN HISTORY AND GENEALOGY DEPARTMENT

Russell Gulch, Colorado, was named for William Greeneberry Russell, a miner from Georgia. With his brothers, he journeyed to Colorado in 1858 and found gold in what soon became the city of Auraria along the banks of Cherry Creek. In June 1859 Russell discovered placer gold deposits in the valley that now bears his name, about two miles southwest of Central City. By the end of the year, hundreds of miners filled the short-lived town of Russell Gulch. Davis's *Barroom Brawl* is a scene typical of many such frontier camps. It is now a ghost town.

SANGRE DE CRISTO LAND GRANT— "TAKING POSSESSION OF THE GRANT"

DRAWING WITH GOUACHE PAINTING, DENVER PUBLIC LIBRARY WESTERN HISTORY AND GENEALOGY DEPARTMENT

This image likely portrays former territorial governor William Gilpin taking possession of his purchase of the Sangre de Cristo Land Grant, in Colorado's San Luis Valley. He bought it from Charles Beaubien in 1863.

H.D.

GEORGE C. SCHLEIER HOME, DENVER

WATERCOLOR AND GOUACHE, 1941, DENVER PUBLIC
LIBRARY WESTERN HISTORY AND GENEALOGY
DEPARTMENT. PUBLISHED IN THE *ROCKY MOUNTAIN
NEWS*, MARCH 9, 1941.

The George C. Schleier residence at 1665 Grant Street
at the southwest corner of East 1st Avenue in Capitol
Hill, is one of the finest designs by Frank Edbrooke,
the leading architect of Denver's late-nineteenth-
century boom years. Edbrooke's client, George
C. Schleier, was a pioneer originally from Baden,
Germany. His early successes came as a hat maker in
Cincinnati, New York, and Milwaukee. Schleier built
one of the first two-story houses in the new settlement
of Denver in 1858. Beginning in 1860, he invested in
freighting in the Denver area and farmed on Cherry
Creek until the flood in 1864, but his biggest successes
in Colorado came from real estate.

Built in 1887 of Colorado sandstone in Queen
Anne style with eclectic elements, the Schleier
mansion occupied a prominent corner location
overlooking downtown Denver. Schleier's heritage is reflected in the home's Germanic details.
The stairway features carvings of gargoyles and
Bavarian swans, which symbolized good luck
for the Germans. The baluster has detailed hand
carvings, and the plynth block on the woodwork,
halfway up from the baseboards, is also common
to German styling. The house was listed on the
National Register of Historic Places in 1977.

THOMAS SKERRITT RANCH, ENGLEWOOD, COLORADO

WATERCOLOR AND GOUACHE, 1940, DENVER PUBLIC LIBRARY WESTERN HISTORY AND GENEALOGY DEPARTMENT. PUBLISHED IN THE *ROCKY MOUNTAIN NEWS*, OCTOBER 13, 1940.

The farmhouse at 3560 South Bannock Street was constructed by Thomas Skerritt, considered the "father" of Englewood. Originally from Ireland, Skerritt emigrated at age twenty, living for periods of time in Michigan, Canada, Chicago, and Leavenworth, Kansas. With his wife, Mary K. Skerritt, he came to Colorado on a wagon train in 1858. After time spent living in Central City and then farming along the South Platte River, Skerritt obtained the land on which the house was built. Skerritt laid out present-day South Broadway Avenue from Cherry Creek to the new town of Englewood by locking the back wheels of a wagon and making the trail along the prairie, taking three trips to sufficiently indent the soil so the trail could be followed.

The two-story frame building with bay windows and a porch was built circa 1870 and remained the Skerritt family home until 1943. Later alterations to the interior made it a multi-family apartment home. The building was determined eligible for the National Register of Historic Places in 2001. After narrowly escaping demolition, it has been restored for office use.

JEFFERSON RANDOLPH "SOAPY" SMITH'S OFFICE AT 17TH & LARIMER

WATERCOLOR AND GOUACHE PAINTING, 1941, DENVER PUBLIC LIBRARY WESTERN HISTORY AND GENEALOGY DEPARTMENT. PUBLISHED IN THE *ROCKY MOUNTAIN NEWS*, MARCH 16, 1941.

The address 1701 Larimer was once the site of Soapy Smith's headquarters. Smith (1860–98) was a famous con artist, saloon and gambling-house proprietor, gangster, and crime boss operating in Leadville, Creede, Denver, and Skagway, Alaska. He was shot and killed in Skagway by vigilantes.

"SUMMER WHITE HOUSE" AT MOUNT FALCON, JEFFERSON COUNTY, COLORADO

WATERCOLOR AND GOUACHE, 1940, DENVER PUBLIC LIBRARY WESTERN HISTORY AND GENEALOGY DEPARTMENT. PUBLISHED IN THE *ROCKY MOUNTAIN NEWS*, NOVEMBER 10, 1940.

John Brisben Walker made a fortune on land speculation in West Virginia and as the publisher of *Cosmopolitan* magazine. In 1879 Walker was appointed by the US Department of Agriculture to investigate the potential for farming in the "arid West." He moved to Colorado, and by the early 1890s he had purchased over 4,000 acres on Mount Falcon, which rises over the town of Morrison in Jefferson County. He attempted to develop the area as a tourist destination, sponsoring the first performances at what is now known as the Red Rocks Amphitheatre. Walker built a grand mansion for his family on Mount Falcon and decided to build a summer residence for the presidents of the United States

on a ridge to the east of his home. Thousands of Colorado schoolchildren donated ten cents each to help finance Walker's dream. A Colorado Yule marble cornerstone inscribed with the words "Summer Home for the Presidents of the United States, Gift from the People of Colorado, 1911" was laid as construction began. But Walker's large investment in the Stanley Steamer Company backfired when the gasoline engine made steam power obsolete, draining Walker's resources. President Woodrow Wilson ignored pleas for federal funding, and Walker, beset by troubles, gave up on the Summer White House. Herndon Davis's painting captures the melancholy in the abandoned ruins of Walker's dream.

TABOR BLOCK, 16TH & LARIMER, DENVER

PENCIL AND WATERCOLOR, 1941, DENVER PUBLIC
LIBRARY WESTERN HISTORY AND GENEALOGY
DEPARTMENT. PUBLISHED IN THE *ROCKY MOUNTAIN
NEWS*, APRIL 27, 1941.

Silver magnate Horace Tabor hired brothers
Willoughby and Frank E. Edbrooke to design this
1879 structure as the finest office building in Denver,
complete with the city's first elevator and telephone
exchange. The building originally housed the First
National Bank and other top businesses. Its decline
is reflected in Davis's watercolor. In 1972 the building fell to the Denver Urban Renewal Authority's
wrecking ball.

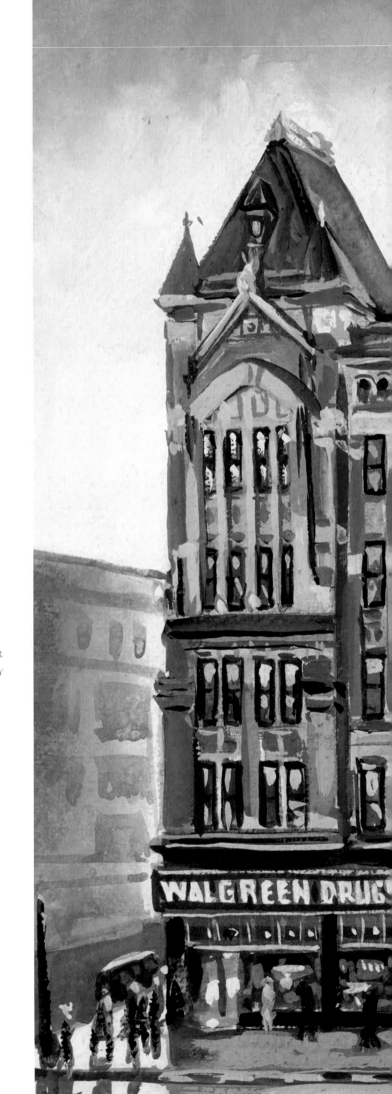

TABOR GRAND OPERA HOUSE, DENVER

WATERCOLOR AND GOUACHE PAINTING, 1941, DENVER
PUBLIC LIBRARY WESTERN HISTORY AND GENEALOGY
DEPARTMENT. PUBLISHED IN THE *ROCKY MOUNTAIN
NEWS*, MARCH 30, 1941.

On 16th Street at the southwest corner of Curtis
Street, silver tycoon Horace Tabor had architects Willoughby and Frank E. Edbrooke design
the most elegant building Denver has ever seen.
Tabor complained that Denver was not building
good buildings and set out to make this one a
pacesetter. After its completion in 1881, the Tabor
Grand brought in celebrated performers such as
Oscar Wilde, Emma Abbott, Helen Modjeska, and
the world's most famous singer-actress, Sarah
Bernhardt. During the 1920s the Tabor became a
movie house. The Tabor was demolished in 1964.
The Federal Reserve Bank now sits on the site.

"ATTACK ON TAOS MISSION," NEW MEXICO

PEN DRAWING, DENVER PUBLIC LIBRARY WESTERN HISTORY AND GENEALOGY DEPARTMENT

This drawing portrays an incident of the Taos Revolt in January 1847, when Mexicans and their Pueblo allies rose up against the US takeover of northern New Mexico during the Mexican-American War. Taos Pueblo women and children sought refuge in the Pueblo church St. Jerome, but the US Army burned down the church and slaughtered those seeking sanctuary there in retaliation for the murder of Governor Charles Bent.

TRIBUNE BUILDING, DENVER

WATERCOLOR, 1940, DENVER PUBLIC LIBRARY WESTERN HISTORY AND GENEALOGY DEPARTMENT. PUBLISHED IN THE *ROCKY MOUNTAIN NEWS*, AUGUST 4, 1940.

This Tribune Building at 1600 Market Street housed the *Denver Tribune*, published from 1871 until 1884, when it became the *Weekly Tribune-Republican*, which lasted until 1886. Eugene Field, the famous journalist, wit, and poet, was managing editor of the *Denver Tribune* between 1881 and 1883.

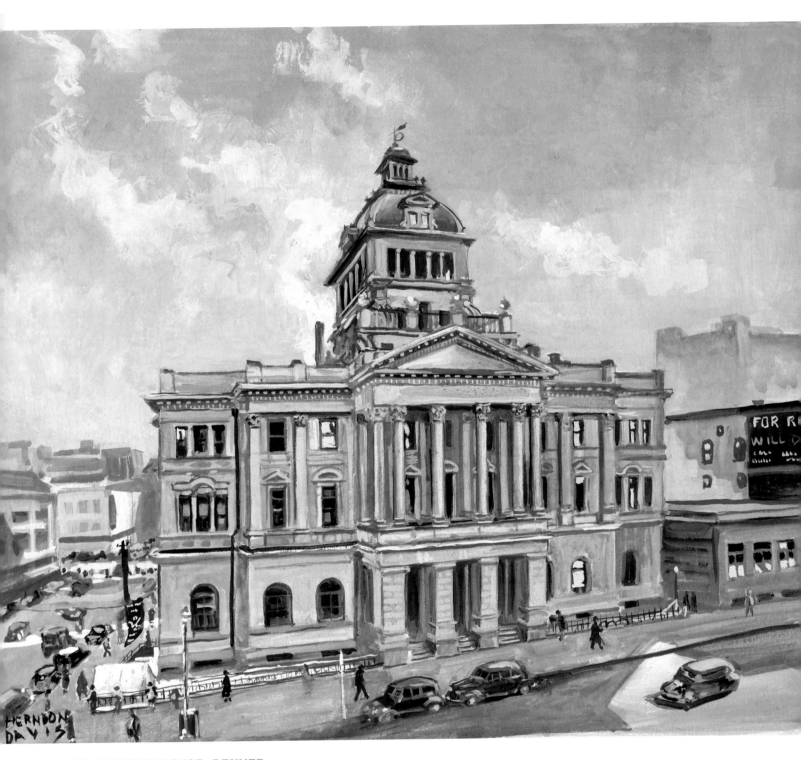

US CUSTOMS HOUSE, DENVER

WATERCOLOR AND GOUACHE, 1941, DENVER PUBLIC LIBRARY WESTERN HISTORY AND GENEALOGY DEPARTMENT. PUBLISHED IN THE *ROCKY MOUNTAIN NEWS*, FEBRUARY 16, 1941.

This watercolor and gouache painting shows the US Customs House at 16th and Arapahoe Streets. The building originally served as both a customs house and a US Post Office, and it became the US Customs House after the post office moved to an even more palatial building at 18th and Stout Streets. This customs house was demolished in 1965. The Federal Reserve Bank now occupies the entire block.

UTE PEAK, COLORADO

PEN DRAWING

The 9,977-foot-high Ute Peak lies in southwestern Colorado. It is sometimes confused with Sleeping Ute Mountain, also on Colorado's southwest corner on the northern edge of the Ute Mountain Ute Reservation. Some say the peak resembles a Ute chief lying on his back with arms folded across his chest. The mountain has long been valued as a sacred place by the Ute Tribe and still plays an important role in their ceremonies. Ute legends have it that the giant Sleeping Ute fell asleep, allowing palefaced Spaniards and then Yankees to invade their land. Someday, they say, Sleeping Ute will wake up and chase off all the newcomers.

JOHN BRISBEN WALKER CASTLE, DENVER

WATERCOLOR, 1940, DENVER PUBLIC LIBRARY WESTERN HISTORY AND GENEALOGY DEPARTMENT. PUBLISHED IN THE *ROCKY MOUNTAIN NEWS*, AUGUST 25, 1940.

This three-story stone castle with battlements, a round tower, and an arched entry was originally part of businessman John Brisben Walker's River Front Park, Denver's first amusement park. The park extended from 15th Street to 19th Street along the Platte River, at the approximate location of today's Commons Park. Walker purchased the land and built the castle along 16th Street in 1887, making it the anchor of an entertainment complex that included a one-quarter-mile oval racetrack with a grandstand that could hold 5,000 people. The track hosted horse races, foot races, and even chariot races. Its grounds staged traveling shows and circuses, including Buffalo Bill's Wild West Show, the National Cowboy Tournament Company, and Barnum's Circus. The castle served as an exposition hall and came to be known as "Walker's Castle of Culture and Commerce." Walker sold the park to the City of Denver in 1893. The castle was used for storage until destroyed by fire in 1951.

ROGER WILLIAMS WOODBURY
MANSION, DENVER

WATERCOLOR AND GRAPHITE PAINTING, 1940, DENVER
PUBLIC LIBRARY WESTERN HISTORY AND GENEALOGY
DEPARTMENT. PUBLISHED IN THE *ROCKY MOUNTAIN
NEWS*, SEPTEMBER 1, 1940.

The Roger Williams Woodbury house at 2501
Woodbury Court in the Jefferson Park neighborhood was a Queen Anne style house featuring
covered first- and second-story front porches, a
tower, an eyebrow dormer, a decorative trim, and
a stone base. Woodbury was a New Hampshire
native who rose through the ranks to the level of
captain as a Union soldier during the Civil War,
followed by a stint in journalism. Woodbury went
west to Colorado in the spring of 1866. He panned
for gold in the streams of Summit County until
he went back to newspaper work with the *Golden
Transcript*, the *Denver Daily Tribune*, the *Denver Daily
Times*, and the *Denver Evening Times*. He became
managing editor and proprietor of the *Tribune* until
he sold his interest in 1871 and launched the *Denver
Daily Times* the following year. The Woodbury
Mansion was built in 1889 and demolished in 1958.

WINDSOR HOTEL, DENVER

WATERCOLOR AND GOUACHE, 1941, DENVER PUBLIC LIBRARY WESTERN HISTORY AND GENEALOGY DEPARTMENT. PUBLISHED IN THE *ROCKY MOUNTAIN NEWS*, APRIL 13, 1941.

The Windsor Hotel at 18th and Larimer Streets featured a corner tower and a mansard roof. Denver's first luxury hotel, the Windsor opened on June 23, 1880. Built with Fort Collins sandstone and rhyolite from Castle Rock, the Second Empire style, five-story Windsor was supposedly modeled after England's Windsor Castle and the Windsor Hotel in Montreal, which claimed at that time to be the largest hotel in the world. The building was financed by an English syndicate calling itself the Denver Mansion Company, Ltd. The hotel's main entrance was on Larimer Street, while a special "ladies' entrance" faced 18th Street.

The Windsor represented the height of luxury in Denver and symbolized the city's growth from a dusty trail stop to a first-class city. Three tunnels supposedly led from the building—one to Union Station, one to a car barn on Arapahoe Street, and the third to palatial marble baths in the neighboring Barclay Block. The Windsor was renowned for fine cuisine, much of which came from its own farm, the Windsor Farm Dairy, complete with imported cows. The Windsor even boasted its own hunters, who brought in wild game. The fine wine cellar was stocked by bartender Harry Tammen, later the founder and proprietor of the *Denver Post* with his partner, Frederick Bonfils. The hotel's Bonanza Bar

featured wall murals of famous figures in Denver's history by artist Herndon Davis. When the building was demolished in 1960, the murals were rescued and eventually relocated to the Sage Room of the Oxford Hotel.

Silver king Horace Tabor, one of the Windsor's owners, kept his mistress, Elizabeth "Baby Doe" McCourt, in the hotel's finest luxury suite. The Tabor Suite supposedly featured a gold leaf bathtub, a 1,500-pound bed and matching dresser of hand-carved walnut, and an Italian marble fireplace. The Windsor also boasted a "floating" grand ballroom with a white ash and black walnut dance floor suspended at each end by cables. The glory days ended when Tabor lost his fortune in the Silver crash of 1893, and he died in one of the hotel's smaller rooms, Room 305, in 1899.

The opening of the Brown Palace Hotel in 1892 and the new Colorado State Capitol building in 1894 moved the center of downtown Denver activity away from Larimer Street, and the area began a steep decline that continued for decades. By the 1930s, the Windsor was "the only flophouse in the world with a marble fireplace in every room." A revival of the Windsor's status in the 1940s was short-lived, and in 1960 the hotel fell to the wrecking ball.

DIPLODOCUS

WATERCOLOR, 1961, DENVER PUBLIC LIBRARY WESTERN
HISTORY AND GENEALOGY DEPARTMENT. ILLUSTRATION
CREATED FOR *HISTORY OF RED ROCKS PARK AND
THEATER* BY NOLIE MUMEY.

Diplodocus was a large plant-eating sauropod from
the Jurassic period whose bones and other dinosaur
fossils were found in the vicinity of Red Rocks Park.

STEGOSAURUS

WATERCOLOR, 1961, DENVER PUBLIC LIBRARY WESTERN HISTORY AND GENEALOGY DEPARTMENT. ILLUSTRATION CREATED FOR *HISTORY OF RED ROCKS PARK AND THEATER* BY NOLIE MUMEY.

A *Stegosaurus* fossil was discovered by Professor Arthur Lakes at Morrison, Colorado, near the current site of Red Rocks Amphitheatre. In 1982, a fourth-grade class at McElwain Elementary School in Thornton, a Denver suburb, persuaded governor Richard D. Lamm to declare *Stegosaurus* the official state fossil.

TRACHODON

WATERCOLOR, 1961, DENVER PUBLIC LIBRARY WESTERN HISTORY AND GENEALOGY DEPARTMENT. ILLUSTRATION CREATED FOR *HISTORY OF RED ROCKS PARK AND THEATER* BY NOLIE MUMEY.

Trachodon is a genus—now considered dubious—of *Hadrosaurid* dinosaur. This classification has been virtually abandoned by modern dinosaur paleontologists.

MAZZULLA MURALS

Fred Mazzulla, a Denver attorney, historian, and
friend of Herndon Davis, commissioned murals
of prominent Coloradans for the basement of his
residence at 1930 East Eighth Avenue in Denver's
Cheesman Park neighborhood. The portraits include
David H. Moffat, John Evans, William Byers, William
M. Gilpin, Joseph P. Machebeuf, Thomas Walsh, and
Buffalo Bill Cody. Cattle brands complete the decor.
Here, Governor Ralph L. Carr and Fred Mazzulla
pose in front of the Herndon Davis portraits.

PRUNES THE BURRO

PAINTING, HISTORY COLORADO

This animal hero is celebrated in the center of the mining town Fairplay, Colorado, with the Prunes Memorial (ca. 1930), a monument of rocks framing a memorial case and bas-relief of a burro that lived to be sixty-three years old. The monument is a tribute to the beasts of burden that hauled materials into remote mining camps and brought out ore.

WINDSOR HOTEL PORTRAIT PANEL

From 1937 to 1946, Herndon Davis frequented the bar at Larimer Street's Windsor Hotel and painted portraits of famous Colorado pioneers in a mural for the bar. When the Windsor fell into decay and was razed in 1960, Davis's work was rescued and ultimately transferred to the Sage Room of the nearby Oxford Hotel. The mural depicts seven prominent figures in Colorado's history: John F. Campion (Leadville silver miner and president of the Denver Chamber of Commerce in 1898), Henry R. Wolcott (a financier who brought outside capital to Denver), Eugene Field (editor of the *Denver Tribune*), Frederick Bonfils (co-owner and publisher of the *Denver Post*), William Byers (founding editor of the *Rocky Mountain News*), Casimiro Barela (a prominent rancher and state senator from Trinidad who helped write the Colorado Constitution), and Otto Mears (a pioneer road and railroad builder in southwestern Colorado).

1. Ernie Pyle quoted in William Barker, "The Life and Times of Herndon Davis," *Rocky Mountain Life* 1, no. 5 (August 1946), 18.

2. Reena Shesso and the Savageau Gallery, *Herndon Davis* (Denver: Denver Public Library Western History and Genealogy Department Archives, 2001), 1.

3. Barker, "Life and Times of Herndon Davis," 18.

4. James, W. Nikl, *Herndon Davis the Artist* (Lakewood, CO: Self-published, 1978), 4.

5. Florence Jackson Stoddard to Herndon Davis, July 26, 1926, Herndon Richard Davis Papers, 1901–62, File Folder 23 (Denver: Denver Public Library Western History and Genealogy Department Archives).

6. *New York Evening Post*, December 8, 1926, 1.

7. *St. Louis Globe Democrat*, August 16, 1927.

8. I. J. Phillipson to G. V. Heidt, May 21, 1927, Herndon Richard Davis Papers, 1901–62, File Folder 23 (Denver: Denver Public Library Western History and Genealogy Department Archives).

9. General J. H. McRae to Herndon Davis, November 29, 1927, Herndon Richard Davis Papers, 1901–62, File Folder 23 (Denver: Denver Public Library Western History and Genealogy Department Archives).

10. G. V. Heidt to Herndon Davis, October 29, 1928, Herndon Richard Davis Papers, 1901–62, File Folder 1 (Denver: Denver Public Library Western History and Genealogy Department Archives).

11. "Yampa Canyon, America's Last Bit of Wild West," *Washington Post*, May 5, 1935, 4.

12. Ibid.

13. *Washington Post*, November 16, 1934, 11.

14. *Denver Post*, December 19, 1954, 6aa.

15. Ibid.

16. Shesso and the Savageau Gallery, *Herndon Davis*, 2; Fred Mazzulla cited by Robert L. Brown in *Central City and Gilpin County: Then and Now* (Lincoln: University of Nebraska Press, 1994), 188–89. Brown gives the name of Davis's young accomplice as Jim Librizzo.

17. Barker, "Life and Times of Herndon Davis," 18.

18. Brown, *Central City and Gilpin County*, 189.

19. Teller Ammons to Herndon Davis, May 26, 1938, Herndon Richard Davis Papers, 1901–62, File Folder 36 (Denver: Denver Public Library Western History and Genealogy Department Archives).

20. Nikl, *Herndon Davis the Artist*, 7.

21. Shesso and the Savageau Gallery, *Herndon Davis*, 3.

22. Nikl, *Herndon Davis the Artist*, 7.

23. Ibid., 8.

24. Mike Flanagan, "Out West," *Denver Post Magazine*, February 10, 1985, 18.

25. Nikl, *Herndon Davis the Artist*, 5.

26. Ibid., 7.

27. Barker, "Life and Times of Herndon Davis," 18.

28. "The Oxford Hotel: The Art and History of a Denver Landmark," http://www.theoxfordhotel.com/wp-content/uploads/2014/07/art-hist3.pdf.

29. Amanda Covarrubias, "Davis Mural Survives Remodeling," *Rocky Mountain News*, June 15, 1988, 8.

30. Herndon Davis, "Photo Murals on Walls of Fred Mazzulla's Basement" (Denver Public Library Digital Collections, 1940–47), http://digital.denverlibrary.org/cdm/search/searchterm/Davis,%20Herndon%20Richard,%201901-1962./mode/exact.

31. "The Herndon Davis Room" (Denver Press Club), http://dpc.connectworkz.com/club-legacy/rooms/the-herndon-davis-room (page removed).

32. Tom Pade, *Herndon Davis: Hidden Treasures* (video) (Denver: Tom Pade, 1999).

33. "Panama to Have Series of Portraits of Popes by American Artist," *New York Times*, December 12, 1954.

34. *Denver Post*, February 18, 1957.

35. Robert L. Perkin, "Herndon Davis Funeral Set Here," *Rocky Mountain News*, November 9, 1962, 14.

36. Frances Melrose, "Face on Barroom Floor Model Dies in Denver Home at 85," *Rocky Mountain News*, November 4, 1975, 5.

Barker, William. "The Life and Times of Herndon Davis." *Rocky Mountain Life* 1, no. 5 (August 1946): 18–19.

Brown, Robert L. *Central City and Gilpin County: Then and Now*. Lincoln: University of Nebraska Press, 1994.

Clark, Alexandra Walker. *Colorado's Historic Hotels*. Charleston, SC: History Press, 2011.

Davis, Herndon Richard. Denver Public Library Digital Archive, 1901–62. http://digital.denverlibrary.org/cdm/search/searchterm/Davis,%20Herndon%20Richard,%201901-1962./mode/exact.

Davis, Herndon Richard. Herndon Richard Papers. Denver: Denver Public Library Western History and Genealogy Department Archives, 1901–62.

Motian-Meadows, Mary, and Georgia Garnsey. *The Murals of Colorado: Walls That Speak*. Boulder: Johnson Books, 2012.

Mumey, Nolie. *History of Red Rocks Park and Theater*. Boulder: Johnson, 1962.

Nikl, James W. *Herndon Davis the Artist*. Lakewood, CO: Self-published, 1978.

Noel, Thomas J. *Buildings of Colorado*. New York: Oxford University Press, 1997.

Noel, Thomas J. *Denver's Larimer Street*. Denver: Historic Denver, 1981.

The Oxford Hotel: The Art and History of a Denver Landmark. http://www.theoxfordhotel.com/wp-content/uploads/2014/07/art-history3.pdf.

Pade, Tom. *Herndon Davis: Hidden Treasures*. Video. Denver: Tom Pade, 1999.

Shesso, Reena, and the Savageau Gallery. *Herndon Davis*. Denver: Denver Public Library Western History and Genealogy Department Archives, 2001.

Wolle, Muriel Sibell. *Stampede the Timberline: The Ghost Towns and Mining Camps of Colorado*. Chicago: Sage Books, 1949.

CRAIG W. LEAVITT is a graduate of the Public History and Preservation Program at the University of Colorado Denver, a former Koch fellow at History Colorado, and the Center for Colorado and the West (CC&W) at the Auraria Library fellow. He has published in History Colorado's *Colorado Heritage* magazine a history of Wink's Lodge, a mountain resort built by and for African Americans in Pinecliffe during the early-twentieth-century segregation era. With CC&W Craig has coauthored a book chronicling the history of the Hilltop Heritage Association, a Denver group that prevented the destruction of their neighborhood's character by rampant real estate development. His publications include an essay on Denver native Neal Cassady, included in the Routledge Press anthology *Across the Great Divide: Cultures of Manhood in the American West,* and an analysis of folk singer Woody Guthrie's place in western US history, published in the University of Colorado Denver's *Historical Studies Journal.* Craig served as chief editor of the 2012 and 2013 editions of the *Historical Studies Journal.* He is also the coauthor of *Colorado Newspapers: A History and Inventory, 1859–2000,* published by CC&W at the Auraria Library and the Colorado Press Association.

THOMAS JACOB NOEL is a professor of history and director of History, Preservation and Colorado Studies at the University of Colorado Denver. He is also co-director of the Center for Colorado and the West at the Auraria Library. Tom is the author or coauthor of forty-four books and hundreds of articles. He appears regularly as "Dr. Colorado" on Channel 9's *Colorado and Company* and writes a column for the Sunday *Denver Post.* Tom completed his MA and PhD at CU-Boulder and has taught at the University of Colorado Denver since 1977. Tom co-edits the *Colorado Book Review,* an online review at coloradowest.auraria.edu /book-reviews. Please check Tom's website, dr-colorado.com, for a full résumé and updated list of his books, classes, tours, and talks.